Energy Healing
in Focus

Energy Healing
in Focus

Des Hynes

To Jim
BEST WISHES
WITH
LOVE AND COMPASSION

DES HYNES

ZAMBEZI PUBLISHING LTD
www.zampub.com

First published in 2017 in the UK by Zambezi Publishing Ltd
Plymouth, Devon PL2 2EQ (UK)
Tel: +44 (0)1752 367 300   Fax: +44 (0)1752 350 453
email: info@zampub.com   www.zampub.com

British Library Cataloguing in Publication Data:
A catalogue record for this book is available from the British Library

ISBN(13) 978-1-903065-87-7
Illustrations copyright © 2017 Jan Budkowski,
Adobe Stock Images and others
Typesetting by Zambezi Publishing Ltd, Plymouth
Printed in the UK by Lightning Source UK

About the Author

Des Hynes is a Usui Holy Fire Reiki Master / Teacher and Psychic Counsellor. He was born in Dublin in 1950. After leaving school at the age of fourteen, he worked in a factory making Morris Minor Cars, and later on as a barman, sometimes working in the most deprived parts of Dublin City.

At the age of 20, he joined the Royal Navy as a Stoker. During the next 30 years, he literally sailed all around the world. After leaving the Navy, Des studied to become a certified accountant. During his wife's illness with cancer, he became interested in energy healing - he noticed how she managed to cope with the side effects of chemotherapy after she had a Reiki Session. Nevertheless, after battling the illness for four years, his wife passed away.

Des understands people on a deep level, and his desire to help people with love and compassion is his driving force. This is his second book on healing energy; his first book, "Do You Really Want to Be Healed?" is also available from Stellium Publishing Ltd. He has two grown up children and five grandchildren. Des lives in Plymouth in Devon and manages to find time to enjoy his favourite pastime as a talented artist.

Dedication
To the memory of my Mother and Father

Contents

Energy Healing:
an Introduction

Energy Healing in Focus

We all have the ability to heal, and healing is a service that we can give to our fellow beings, be they human or animal. As with most things in life, some people are better at healing than others, although with hard work and practice we can all give some form of healing. Motivation is everything, because the more you put into it and the more you practise, the better your healing energy will flow.

There is energy in everything, from stones and plants to animals and humans, although the energy in a rock vibrates at a different frequency to the energy in a human, but whatever the form it takes, we are surrounded with this universal life-force energy that sustains life as we know it. The source of all healing comes from same place, so it doesn't matter if you practise Reiki or Spiritual healing, the result will be just as effective.

Healing energy is known by different names, which are Chi in China, Ki in Japan and Prana in India respectively. Rei-Ki is made up from two words (pronounced Ray Kee). The first part, Rei, means universal or divine and higher wisdom. The second part, Ki, refers to the life force energy that flows through all things.

Why do some people want to be healers? There is a divine spark within each one of us, and this divine spark is love and compassion. We are all connected, just as every drop of water in the ocean is connected. When we

Introduction

see someone in physical or mental pain, or perhaps suffering grief for the loss of a loved one, we feel their pain too, because we are at one with them. It is through love and compassion that our instinct operates and gives us the desire to help those who are in pain and to comfort them.

Our physical bodies are made from atoms, and they in turn are made of subatomic particles, protons, neutrons and electrons. Within each human cell the protons have a positive electric charge and the electrons have a negative electric charge and this interaction produces the energy that sustains life. The energy that it produces is called the human energy field. This positive and negative concept isn't unique, because there is a negative (Yin) and positive (Yang) component in everything. A car battery needs a negative charge in addition to a positive charge to produce electricity. Everything about us is made of different types of energy. Nothing is static and everything involves some form of movement or vibration. Our thoughts and feelings are linked to everyone and everything in the universe. It is through this process that we can connect to the suffering of others and that we feel the desire to help, and that we have the ability to do so.

The human body is equipped with amazing and sophisticated healing processes that allow bodies to repair and maintain themselves, as long as we allow them to do so, and research has shown that ninety-eight per cent of the cells in our body are renewed each year. Your liver gradually replaces itself every six weeks, your skin is renewed every month and your stomach lining every four days. Many things can have an effect on this natural regeneration, so we need to eat a healthy balanced diet, drink plenty of water and we should try to avoid stress.

When we cut ourselves, our blood pressure drops in order to decrease the amount of blood loss, and the wound will then form a protective cover (scab) under which the healing takes place. I have seen a large open wound the size of a large man's hand, which was too big to take stitches heal, and all that was required was a sterile dressing to prevent infection. If we break a bone in our arm or leg, all that is required is for the bone to be set and immobilized, because the body's repair system will do the rest.

To facilitate this healing there are some things we need to do, because just as we must look after the engine of a car, we need to look after our bodies. Putting the right food into our bodies is as necessary as putting the correct fuel and oil into a car engine if it is to achieve optimum performance.

As a child growing up in the early nineteen fifties in Dublin we were always getting sick, and runny noses and coughs were the normal par for the course, but it was only when I got older that I realized that it was the lack of nutritious food, combined with cold and damp living conditions that had made us susceptible to illness. We lived in a three-room cottage with a coal fire in the living room and this was well before the days of central heating and double glazing, so when we went to bed in winter, there would be ice on the inside of the window pane. To supplement our lack of a healthy diet we had daily doses of cod liver oil, and even today I prefer the bottled cod liver oil to the capsules.

Introduction

To say that people like you and I are healers is a misconception, because the reality is that it is not we who achieve the healing, as we only set the scene and create the conditions that allow the body and mind to do the healing. It is becoming more popular today for people to question the health care provided by doctors within the medical profession, and it might surprise you to know that it is the older generation that is more inclined towards holistic healing.

When we were young we thought that the doctor had power over life and death and we trusted him completely. It was a blind trust that we did not question. Today things have changed, and younger people entering the medical profession are more willing to accept that, "There are more things in heaven and earth, Horatio, then are dreamt of in your philosophy".

Some hospitals are giving Energy Healing in the form of Reiki to cancer patients to help with the side effects of chemotherapy. In my case, it was while my wife was being treated for cancer that I became interested in Reiki, because I noticed how calm and contented she was after having a Reiki session.

If we go to the doctor, we feel disappointed if we don't come away with a prescription for pills or lotions. How would you feel if the doctor told you to rest and to stop eating for a few days? When we eat, the body has to use energy to digest the food, so by fasting and drinking plenty of water, that energy is redirected to the healing of our illnesses.

Energy Healing in Focus

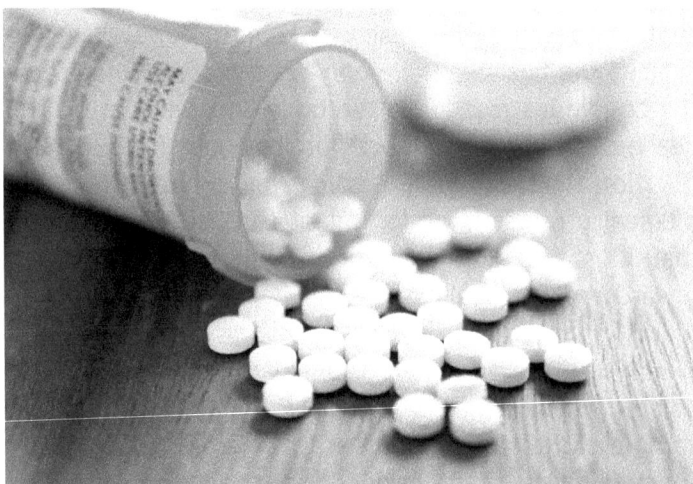

It's true that western medication tends to treat the symptoms of the illness whereas holistic healing treats the cause.

Energy Healing treats the mind body and soul. Our real self or soul is perfect, without any form of illness, so the real you and the real me are in mint condition without any flaws or problems. By using Energy Healing we can re-align our physical body and mind with our true selves, and everyone is entitled to be happy and healthy. Also, if we don't remove the cause, there is a good chance that the problem will return at a later date.

Illness happens when we are out of balance with our true selves, so we need to deal with the cause as well as the condition that manifests as the illness. The cause may be due to the toxic environment in which we live, exposure to germs, bacteria and viruses. It might even be in our genetics. We can also make ourselves sick by the kind of work we do, by physical discomfort and by stress due to worry or anger. Irrespective of what it is that needs to be healed, we have to identify the cause to ensure a permanent solution is achieved.

All fresh fruit, salads and vegetables should be washed before eating, even when they are organic, because there is more than chemicals that can land up on the produce during the picking and packing process.

One: Energy

There is energy in everything from the smallest atom in our body to the sun that shines in the sky. Though we may not see it, we know that energy exists, just like the air we breathe and the electricity we use every day. We can't see it but know it's there. In healing, we work mainly with the following types of energy.

Earth Energy

Earth energy is the energy from the earth below, which includes the food we eat and the environment that surrounds us. The forests have been described as the lungs of the planet, because they absorb toxins from the air that we breathe. The outer core or crust of our planet earth reaches down about two thirds of the way to the centre of the earth, and the inner core is an inhospitable place that comprises molten iron with a pressure that is 3.5 million times the pressure of the surface. The temperature at the core of the earth is about as hot as the surface of the sun. There is some speculation that the combination of such high temperatures and pressure might even have resulted in a large crystal forming at the very centre of our planet. This would not surprise me, as crystals are widely known for the energy they emit and they are frequently used for various types of holistic healing.

Crystal Energy

Bloodstone crystals are dark green with red flecks, and they are particularly good for grounding purposes. I use them at the end of a Reiki healing session to ground or connect the client to the earth, because it is important for a person to be grounded when giving or receiving Energy Healing. When you receive healing your Chakras are opened to receive the flow of energy. Your Crown Chakra is where the cosmic energy enters the body and this connects you with your higher self or soul. Though this brings a lovely feeling of peace and tranquillity when healing takes place, it isn't practical to walk around with this Chakra being open and energised, because we need to live in the real world.

Once I was giving a healing session to a lady, and I forgot to ground her properly after the session. The next time I spoke to this lady she said how much the healing had helped her, but she couldn't get to sleep till three o'clock in the mornings. This was because her Crown Chakra was still open, and her feet and Base Chakra were not connected to the earth. Needless to say, I gave her a grounding treatment and she was fine after that.

On another occasion I placed two bloodstone crystals on either side of a client's feet to ground her after a session, but when it was time for her to leave, she said she could not move her feet and could I please remove the crystals!

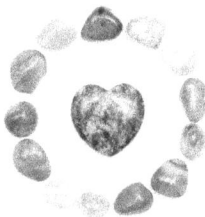

I had another client who, when I was about to give a healing session, put her hand down her jumper and brought out a handful of crystals, which she told me she always carried around in her bra for protection!

Nutritional Energy - Water

It is a combination of the earth and the sun that creates the energy that we obtain from our food. The plants draw earth energy through their roots and the sun energy enters into the leaves.

A Hindu Holy man by the name of Prahlad Jani is reputed to have had nothing to eat or drink for 70 years. For the last 40 years he has lived a hermit-like existence in a cave in the jungle. He spends most of the day meditating and he can meditate for periods up to twelve hours at a time. He is a follower of the Hindu Goddess Amba, who he believes feeds him with a life-giving invisible energy that allows him to live without food or water. To test his claim, he was kept in the "Sterling Hospital" in Ahmedabad for fifteen days, where he was monitored around the clock. He did not eat or drink during this period. At the end of the fifteen days, doctors carried out tests and said he was fit and healthy.

One morning I went to my bathroom and noticed a puddle of water on the floor just under the place where I keep a large plant. I hadn't watered the plant for some time, so that couldn't be the cause of the puddle – or could it? On closer inspection I noticed a drop of water at the end of a leaf that was sticking out from the side of the plant, and I could see that the plant was absorbing moisture from the air in the bathroom whenever the temperature dropped back after I had bathed. This could explain how cactus plants manage to survive in the desert for years on end without much rain.

We do not drink enough water. Our kidneys process 200 quarts of blood daily, sifting out waste and transporting urine to the bladder, so the kidneys need water to flush away the toxins in the body. Water also prevents skin problems, but you should stick to still bottled water, or use a filter if drinking tap water. Another idea is to leave a jug of tap water in the fridge overnight, as that removes some of the impurities.

Nutritional Energy - Food

Another source of earth energy comes from food. Our bodies take the energy and nutrients they require from the food we eat, so it's important that we eat the right foods – ideally fresh food that is free from chemicals and pesticides, so where possible, we should choose organic food.

Pesticides are used to kill the bugs, so in reality if we don't eat organic foodstuffs, we are taking in food that has a layer of poison on it. Packs of fruit, vegetables and salads often tell us to wash the goods before eating them, but that is only to protect the producers from prosecution. Our eating habits are as important as what we eat; if we don't eat enough, our energy becomes depleted, and this results in lowering our resistance to illness. However, overeating is just as bad, because when we overindulge, the body can't break down the food quickly enough. This means that toxins build up, and these toxins - let alone the excess fat that piles up inside us - can harm our bodies.

Energy in the Air

The air we breathe is just as important as the food we eat. It is a fact that a baby born in a more affluent society has a better chance of survival than one born in a deprived area, and it has long been known that removing children from an inner city where the air quality is poor and taking them to the seaside or countryside will improve their health. Those of you who are in the habit of going for early morning walks will notice that the air seems cleaner and more invigorating then than it is later in the day. Air pollution has become a major concern in this day of traffic congestion, although we are moving in the right direction with control of car exhaust emissions.

As a child in the early 1950s, I remember the smog that we suffered during the winters. This was a mixture of coal smoke and dense fog which was often so bad you couldn't see two feet in front of you. The Great Smog of 1952 lasted for seven days, and it was estimated that at least 4,000 people died prematurely and 100,000 more were made ill due to its effects on the human respiratory tract. These so called "pea-soupers" were very thick yellowish, greenish or even black fog which was a direct result of air pollution. The "Clean Air Act" of 1956 was the start of the fight back against this pollution, but today there are still parts of the world that are prone to high air pollution. So it is not just the air we breathe that is important but the quality of that air. Even then, most of us don't breathe correctly; we tend to breath shallowly when we should be taking deep breaths, that's why exercise is so good, because it makes us work harder to fill our lungs with air.

1: Energy

Solar Energy

There is also energy from the cosmos that flows through our universe, and we are beginning to understand the effects that the sun and moon have on our lives. Solar flares can contain high energy photons and particles, and these electromagnetic bursts can affect low-frequency radio communications on earth, in ways that experts call "atmospherics".

The benefits from our sun are well known, and without the sun our planet would die. While this wouldn't be good news for us, when we look at the big picture, the death of our sun would have little impact on the millions of other galaxies in the universe.

Universal or Cosmic Energy

Universal or cosmic energy comes from a source that cannot be explained by modern science. We strive to understand everything and we think we have the ability to achieve that aim, but we are not as clever as we sometimes think we are. Step back and look at the big picture. We cannot comprehend what is beyond infinity... yet we know that everything has a beginning and a finite point. This may be due to our understanding of the way that things work. You would not expect your pet cat or dog to drive a car, as it is beyond their comprehension, so maybe we should accept the fact that there are things beyond our own comprehension.

So universal or cosmic energy is a spiritual energy that surrounds and permeates everything, and this energy comes directly from the "source", which many people call God, the Creator or the Divine. It can be described as the breath of life. Through this energy, we can connect to our higher or real selves. It is important to remember that we are spirit, although in the physical state of being in a human body. When our physical body dies, the soul survives and moves on to the next lesson that we need to learn on our road to spiritual development, and some of this comes through reincarnation. By meditating, we can connect to our real selves and acquire spiritual knowledge.

Healers use this spiritual energy because it transcends all other types of healing, and indeed, the highest vibrational frequency of love heals the body, mind and spirit, through which all things can be healed.

Two: Chakras

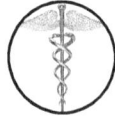

Chakra is a Sanskrit word meaning "wheel" and it refers to each of the seven main centres of energy in the human body. These Chakras are energy transformers that are capable of shifting energy to a higher or lower vibration, or vice-versa. We are not just constructed out of physical matter. We are also made from energy that vibrates at different frequencies and which interacts with the world around us, be it on a physical or spiritual plane. Energy Healing is largely based on working through the Chakras. It is through these that we can diagnose the cause of an ailment and facilitate its healing.

There are seven major Chakras but also twenty-one minor Chakras. For example, the two minor Chakras in the palms of the hands become important when carrying out hands-on healing. On a social note, you have probably noticed that you can get an impression about a person by shaking hands with him.

If our Chakras are balanced and spinning correctly, the flow of universal energy is maintained within and around us, but when blockage occurs in one of the Chakras, the flow of energy is disrupted and illness develops. Energy Healing clears this blockage and repairs any damage that has been done. Each Chakra spins, and while one spins clockwise, the next spins anti-clockwise and so on. Some energy healers use a pendulum to check the rotation and speed of the Chakras. (Incidentally, a wooden pendulum is thought best for this task.)

2: Chakras

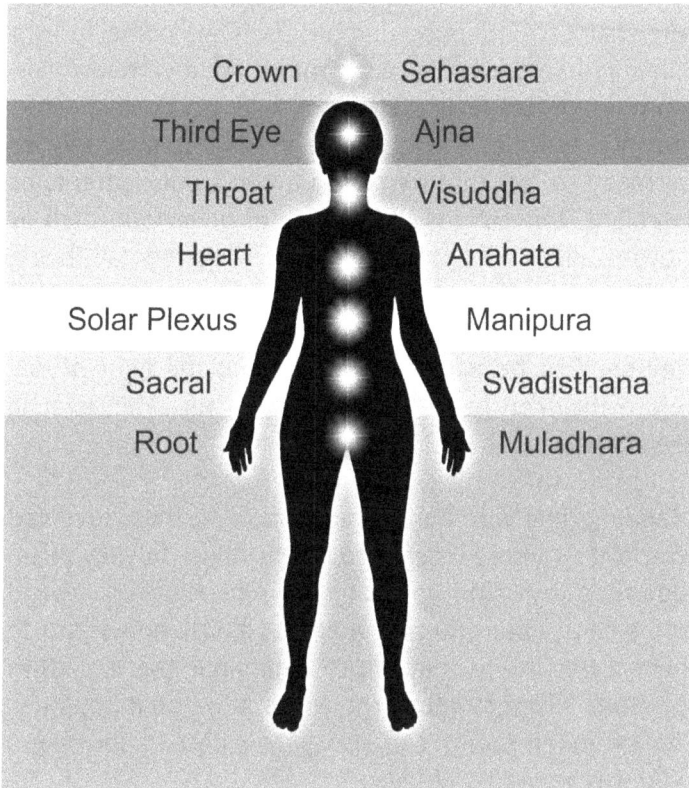

Crown	·	Sahasrara
Third Eye		Ajna
Throat		Visuddha
Heart		Anahata
Solar Plexus		Manipura
Sacral		Svadisthana
Root		Muladhara

The Base Chakra

When we are born, our Chakras are closed, and they open in seven-year cycles starting with the Base Chakra. The Base or root Chakra (Mulhadhara in Hindu) is coloured red and it is situated between the anus and genitals on the perineum.

This Chakra is associated with the material things that we need in order to survive; such as, eating, drinking and shelter. Security and physical well-being are associated with this Chakra, so it is where we get our mental and physical stability from. We rely on others for the first seven years of our life, which makes this a very important time that can influence our future. If we come from a stable and secure background that is filled with love and approval we feel secure, which makes us outgoing, confident and reliable. If we have to fight to survive and we are made to feel that we are a burden to our parents or guardians, this can lead to unhelpful behaviour, such as showing signs of violence, being judgemental, being fearful or needing to accumulate unnecessary material possessions. These negative issues can be healed, but they need to be addressed and shown the light of day before they can be healed. As we will see later, healing needs focus, so it is not just random.

Spending time with our children, showing them love and affection is more useful to them than buying them expensive toys, and you can't buy the time you spend with a child when you take them for a walk or just talk to them. Later in life they won't remember the expensive toys, but will remember the times you spent together. The extended family can also play a part in showing a child it is wanted and loved.

The Sacral Chakra
The Sacral Chakra (Svadisthana in Hindu) is coloured orange, and it is situated below the belly button. It starts to open from the age of seven years and it should be fully open by the age of fourteen. It is also known as the sexual Chakra, which naturally kicks in when puberty starts.

When the Sacral Chakra is balanced, we have harmony in relationships and ease of physical contact with our fellow humans. We learn to share and we are happy in others' company. If it is out of balance we can show symptoms of jealousy, fear of sexuality, uninhibited desire and lack of creative energy. We can help to balance this Chakra in others by giving them confidence and building their self-belief and self-worth as part of society. If a child is worried about a subject in school (this may seem trivial to us but it is a major concern to them) you can highlight the things they are good at, which will turn a negative situation into a positive, and make it half-full instead of being half-empty.

The Solar Plexus Chakra

The Solar Plexus Chakra (Manipura in Hindu) is coloured yellow and it is located above the belly button. This starts to open from the age of fourteen, so this is where we connect to the world we live in. It concerns our relation-ships with others, the way we feel, our emotions and our feeling of belonging. If we upset someone we love and care about, we get that empty feeling of loss or pain in the Solar Plexus.

When this Chakra is balanced, we have an air of authority and we are good at organising things as we have natural leadership qualities. If the Solar Plexus Chakra is out of balance, we can become rebellious and stubborn and we throw our toys out of the pram until we get our own way. It will not surprise most people that this Chakra covers the teenage years.

It is not only children who have problems with the Solar Plexus Chakra. One day a gentleman and his wife came to see me for some Reiki healing. This man had not long retired and he had developed a problem with his hands, so when he tried to do anything with them they would shake uncontrollably. He had been to see the doctor and had endured various tests, but the results indicated that there was nothing physically wrong. What made matters worse was that this man was the secretary of his local hydrangea growing club, so the problem with his hands was affecting his potting capabilities, thus diminishing his ability to indulge in one of his main passions in life.

I started the Reiki treatment as normal, and when I reached the Solar Plexus area my hand got very hot. This was an indication that there was a strong flow to that Chakra, so when the healing was complete I mentioned that there had been a problem in that area, and I asked him if he ever got angry. It was then that he told me that he was taking medication for anger issues. I felt that he was afraid he was losing his prestigious role in the grower's club and this was playing on his ego, but it might have been a side-effect of the medication he was taking. I can only assume the healing did the trick, because he never came back.

The Base, Sacral and Solar Plexus are what could be described as *earth* or *ground* Chakras, because they cover our basic instincts of survival, which are food, shelter and clothing. The upper Chakras are connected to our mental and spiritual development.

The Heart Chakra
The Heart Chakra (Anahata in Hindu) is coloured green and it is situated in the area of the heart. This is where our ability to heal comes from. It is from the heart that we show love and compassion. I expect you have heard the saying, "his heart was not in it". This is very true, for we need to feel love, dedication, unification, openness, spontaneity and warmth in our Heart Chakra. If you have ever lost someone you loved, you will know that feeling of loss

within your heart, and if this Chakra is unbalanced, it will manifest in problems with relationships and emotions. It will make us feel suspicious and we will lack self-love.

You may be surprised at the number of people who don't love themselves. One girl I knew disliked herself so much that she couldn't bear to look at her own reflection in the mirror. There is a difference between loving yourself and vanity, because how can you expect others to love you if you don't love yourself? If you suffer from lack of self-esteem or self-love, you need to look in the mirror every morning and remind yourself how good and kind you are, and accept that everyone is not perfect but everyone is loved. It might be worth repeating the following mantra every day:

All is Love

You are Love

I am Love

Remember, when it comes to Energy Healing, the heart plays a major role: it is where we generate the love and compassion needed to facilitate the healing.

The Throat Chakra

The Throat Chakra (Vishudda in Hindu) is coloured light blue and it is the fifth Chakra. It is situated at the Base of the neck and it is associated with the thyroid grand. This gland affects our growth and metabolism. This Chakra is where we learn to express ourselves; it also governs communication, but not only on a verbal level. If we see something that stirs our emotions or if we hear a piece of emotional music, we get a lump in our throat.

It is where we transform our thoughts into the sound that is required to get our message across, but we communicate through a variety of methods including by intuition. The Throat Chakra's location is between the mind (which sees things in a practical way) and the heart (which relies on emotions), so this sometimes comes into conflict.

This Chakra is linked to wisdom and knowledge, so those who have a balanced Throat Chakra are confident and articulate, while if the Chakra is unbalanced or blocked, people have trouble expressing themselves, and they may also have a tendency to swallow and stammer. They can be easily influenced and misled by others and their creativity can become dampened.

The Third Eye Chakra

The Third Eye Chakra (Ajna in Hindu) is coloured dark blue and it is situated between the eyebrows and behind the eyes (near the pineal gland). This Chakra connects us with our inner vision. It is common when I am giving Reiki healing in the area of the Third Eye for the client to see a bright light like the sun, even though the healing takes place in a dimly lit room. This is where our intuition comes in and it may come in the form of dreams, visions, clairvoyance and telepathy. Visions and spiritual awareness are sometimes preceded by a bright light. When it is open, we get an insight to our spiritual being and we can access occult knowledge. If there is a blockage or imbalance in the Third Eye Chakra, we refuse to learn life's lessons and we can become pessimistic or even confused.

This is also known as the Brow Chakra

2: Chakras

The Crown Chakra
The Crown Chakra (Sahasrara in Hindu) is coloured violet or gold, and it is at the top of the head where the skull bones meet. Just as the Base Chakra connects us with the material world, the Crown Chakra is the gateway to our spiritual enlightenment. It has sometimes been referred to as our "God Source". It is depicted in art as a thousand-petal lotus: the lotus flower being a symbol in both Hindu and Buddhist traditions, as its roots are in muddy waters but the lotus flower blooms in the light.

When we connect to the cosmic consciousness, we feel an inner peace and awareness. An unbalanced or blocked Crown Chakra can manifest in fear or resistance to spiritual progress and this is evident in people who only recognise the material world.

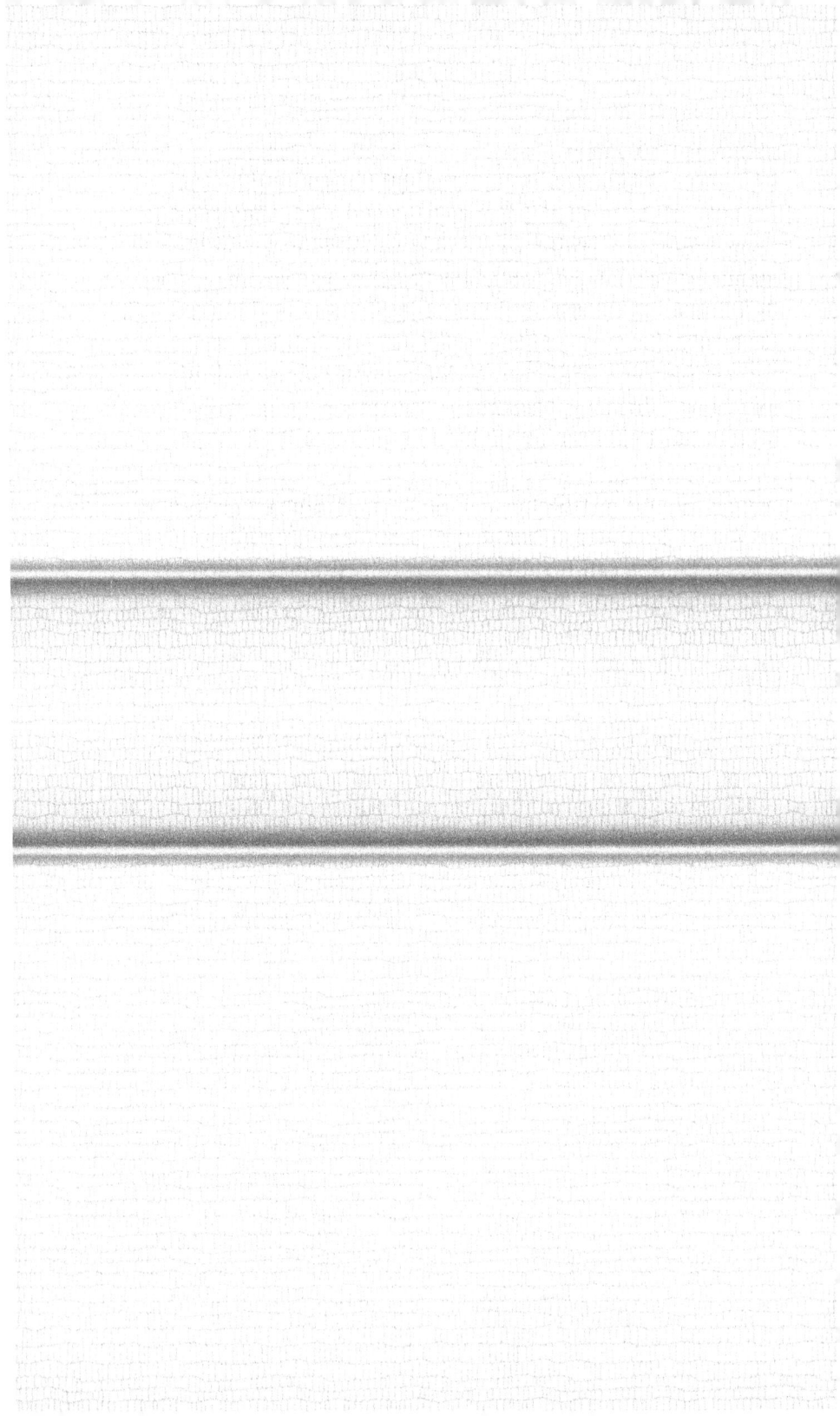

Three: The Aura

Energy Healing in Focus

The aura is an energy field that surrounds the human body and it does so in a form of layers. These energy or auric layers connect us to our surroundings and to the outside world. It is a form of antenna that receives information and which can also be used to transmit our feelings to others. I can remember looking at illustrations of saints and other venerable people depicted in art when I was a child, and they are shown with the glow of a halo around their head. I thought this seemed a bit far-fetched, but one day when I was teaching a Reiki class, one of my students was a lady who we called red-haired Sue. A fellow Reiki master called Angie was demonstrating healing on me while I lay on the therapy couch, when Sue saw a glow of light around Angie's head, and flashes of blue running down her arms from the elbows to the finger tips. Sue also observed blue lights going up and down my body.

Sue is a very gentle and spiritual person who is particularly good at communicating with animals, especially dogs. She told me about a dog she was helping, which was very sad and forlorn. When she made contact with the sad dog, she got a vivid image of the dog biting someone's arm. She couldn't see who the person was, but it was the result of this incident that led to the dog being sad. Sue relayed the information to the dog's owner who confirmed that the dog had bitten the owner's brother and that the wound had required stitches. Sue's love of animals led to her intended desire to use her Reiki to heal animals as well as humans.

3: The Aura

Some people can see auras clearly, but most of us only see them as a haze around the body, especially the head. There is a method of photographing the auras called aura imaging. This is done by the person placing their left hand into a hand sensor. The sensor has various contact points that connect to certain organs of the body, allowing the machine to measure the electromagnetic field of the body, and this is transferred on to an image for detailed analysis. I tried this myself, and when I was attached to the sensor I could see all the colours around my Chakras. As an experiment I thought about a pleasant experience and this resulted in a golden-green aura forming around my heart. Then I thought about something unpleasant from my past, and this showed up as the colour red in my Heart Chakra. Perhaps in future, this type of imagery will become more refined and it may be used in hospitals the same way we use X-rays for diagnostic purposes today.

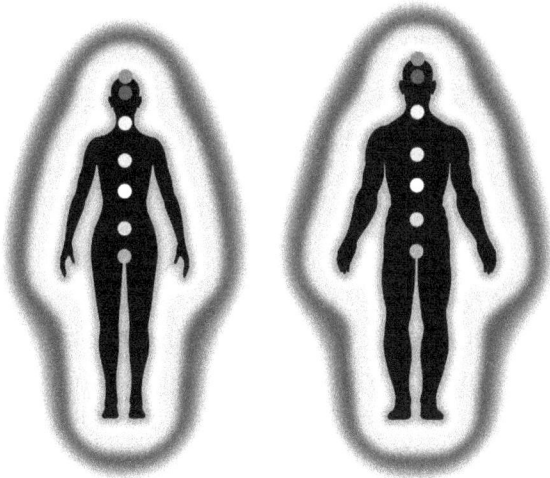

The Physical Auric Body

The aura that is closest to the physical body is the physical auric body, and this is linked to the Base Chakra and therefore, its colour is red. This extends from one quarter to two inches beyond the physical body and it is associated with physical sensations and comfort.

The Etheric Auric Body

The second aura layer is the etheric auric body and is not as dense as the first layer. It is linked to the Sacral Chakra and it is associated with feelings such as love, excitement, joy or anger, this extends between one and three inches from the body and its colour is orange.

The Etheric Layer

The third auric layer is the etheric layer and is finer in density. This connects to the Solar plexus Chakra and it is where our rational mind and thought forms can be observed, which means that if we get angry, it glows with red shades instead of its normal golden yellow colour.

> The first three layers of the aura are called the physical plane

The Astral Level

The fourth auric layer is the astral level. It is at this level where we interact with other people and this layer is connected to the Heart Chakra. We communicate our feelings to those to whom we are attracted through this level, so this is where the energy fields of two people who are compatible talk to each other. Our energies of spiritual growth and love originate here. This layer extends from six inches to one foot from the body and the colour of this aura is green.

The Etheric Template

The fifth layer of the aura is the etheric template and it is linked to the Throat Chakra. It extends up to one-and-a-half feet from the physical body. This is where we feel our uniqueness and identity, but it is also how we connect to the divine aspects of our being, so it guides us to speak and follow the truth. Its colour is light blue.

The Third Eye Aura

The sixth layer of the aura is associated with the Third Eye Chakra. It is from here we can connect to the God or to the Divine, so it is through this aura field that we feel unconditional love, but it also has a group consciousness where we share the divine love. It extends from two to two-and-a-half feet from the body and its colour is dark blue.

This is also known as the Brow Chakra

The Ketheric Template

The seventh layer is the ketheric template and it links with the Crown Chakra. This extends from two-and-a-half feet to three feet from the physical body. The colour purple is seen in this layer of the aura and it is where we connect to our real selves. It denotes the way we fit in with the great scheme of things.

Although the aura normally extends to about three feet from the physical body, it can extend much further, depending on the energy and the spiritual condition of the person. Before you enter a room, your aura may already have connected with those on the other side of the door, and it can lead you to places to which you feel intuitively drawn.

How to See an Aura

This experiment is worth trying. Ask a friend to stand against a plain background, for example a painted wall or one with plain, pale wallpaper on it. Stare at your friend with your eyes slipping out of focus and allow the shape of your friend's head, shoulders and upper body to impinge onto your retina. Ask your friend to keep still while you close your eyes. You will see your friend's outline fairly clearly, but with a bit of luck, you will also start to see colours swirling around the outline. If this doesn't happen straight away, open your eyes, gaze vacantly at your friend again and then close your eyes again. This time, it should work.

Once you have performed this experiment, you will be able to assess what the aura is telling you. For instance, it's unlikely under those circumstances that you will see much red, as that would indicate anger. You should see yellow, which would indicate your friend's desire to learn and her interest in what you are trying to do, along with blue, showing a desire to communicate and green or even pale pink, showing friendship and affection. There may be hints of violet for spirituality, turquoise for healing and many other variations on a theme.

Four: Reiki

Energy Healing in Focus

Meridians

The meridians are the channels or super highways for energy distribution. There are between 400 and 500 access points to these superhighways, which are circuits of positive and negative energies. There are twelve major meridians and several secondary ones. Some of the major meridians connect to the lungs, large intestine, stomach, heart and liver.

The meridians are extensively used in Chinese medicine, because the ancient Chinese considered the body as a whole rather than in separate parts. They see energy as something that flows in a circuit, in a similar manner to that in which the blood flows around the body, and access to this energy circuit is made at the acupressure access points. Acupuncture is a fine art which takes from three to four years to learn, and the Chinese also normally learn herbal medicine to complement their acupuncture skills. Reflexology is another type of healing that uses the meridians, because by massaging certain parts of the feet, the reflexologist can effect healing in the organs.

Principles of Healing

All Reiki healers live by the five Reiki principles set by Dr Mikao Usui, who rediscovered Reiki healing in Japan at the beginning of the twentieth century. When you live by these principles, your life will change for the better.

4: Reiki

The Five Reiki Principles

By Dr Mikao Usui

Just for today, I will let go of anger.

Just for today, I will let go of worry.

Today, I will count my many blessings.

Today, I will do my work honestly.

Today, I will be kind to every Living Creature.

The first principle is:
"Just for today, I will let go of anger".
When we get angry at others or ourselves this creates blockages in our energy fields. By being angry we lose control and give power to others. It is the most complex inner enemy. Letting go of anger brings peace into the mind. Note how we say "Just for today". We do this because we live in the present moment, which means that tomorrow we can recommit ourselves anew. The second principle is "Just for today I will let go of worry". Anger deals with past or present events, but worry deals with the future and carries the "what if" factor. Endless worries fill our heads, so that they become small holes that bore into our body and soul. How many of us can remember what we were worried about this time last year? And furthermore, did worrying about things change anything?

The second principle is:
"Just for today, I will let go of worry".
Some people get worried if everything is going well because their mind starts to invent problems that don't exist. However, people who it is better to avoid are "energy vampires" because they will tell you all their woes, and then say, "I feel much better now", while you, on the other hand, feel drained and ready to do yourself in. The best way to deal with this type of person is to try and change their negative to a positive but if you can't, then you need to learn the art of "listening without listening". Remember, worry does not change things, and it uses up energy that can be more usefully tapped into for healing purposes.

The third principle is:
"Today I will count my many blessings".
No matter how bad things are, there is always something to be grateful for. Perhaps it's the people we love or the simple things that we take for granted that can help to make us feel happy.

The fourth principle is:
"Today, I will do my work honestly".
This means learning to earn a respectable living without harming other people or the environment so that we can support our family. If someone I have to deal with is dishonest, I no longer get upset, because in the long run, they only do harm to themselves owing to the law of karma. Generally speaking though, the vast majority of people are honest.

4: Reiki

The fifth principle is:
"Today, I will be kind to every living creature".
We are all connected through the universal life force energies, whether it be this planet or the cosmos, so with that in mind, some people decide to be vegetarian. While this is commendable, if you don't want to give up meat, then before you eat it, you may wish to give thanks to the animal that has given its life for your benefit.

As I said earlier, healing is a service that we can give to our fellow beings. To serve we have to be prepared metaphorically speaking "to walk without shoes". By this I mean we have to be humble, and oblivious to what others think.

When I was in Dublin in the late sixties and working as an apprentice barman, we had to go to college one morning each week, and part of that education was a period of religious instruction given by a Franciscan monk. He wore a brown habit and had sandals, so even in the harshest of winters when there was ice and snow on the ground, he didn't wear socks or shoes, only sandals. This image has stayed with me and because this monk was a good man, who was clearly guided by the highest of principles, it reminds me that the way in which we conduct our lives and the principles by which we are guided affect the success that we have with our healing.

We all have egos, but some people's self-importance can get in the way when it comes to healing. The best way to heal others is to first heal ourselves, and this can be achieved by letting go of our egos. It is better that others sing our praises than for us to sing them ourselves. Go about your healing with a kind and loving heart without seeking fame or fortune, and help all who need it without judging them.

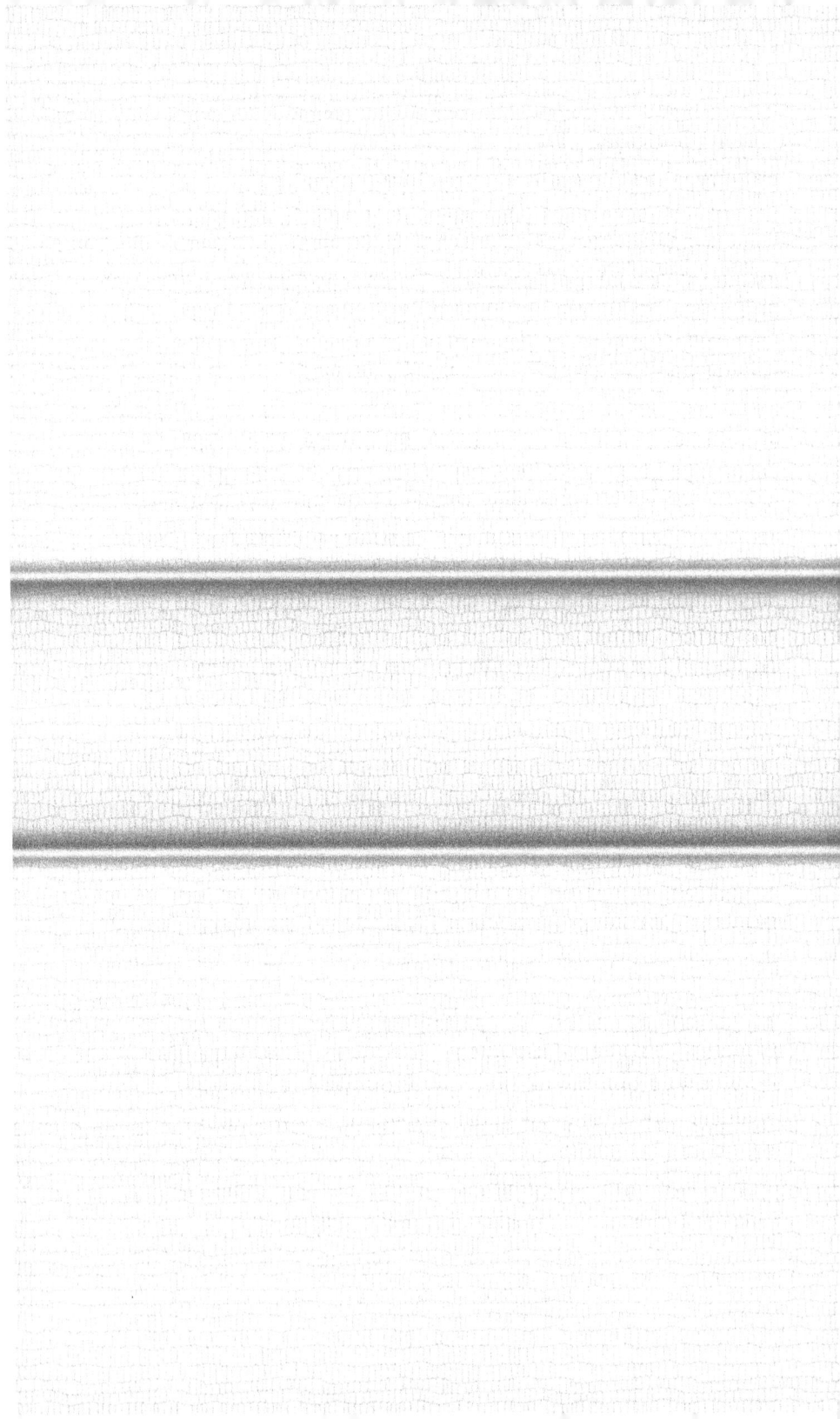

Five: Illnesses and Healing Techniques

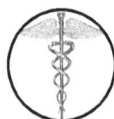

Causes of Illness

There are various types of illness; they may be physical, mental or emotional, and while these are sometimes linked, each can be an individual matter. Mental and emotional illness can lead to a physical illness if it is not treated. For instance, people who worry tend to hunch their shoulders, and this can lead to neck or back pain. The environment in which we live can be a contributing factor, so those who live close to coal mines or steel works where toxic fumes bellow out into the atmosphere, tend to suffer with chest and breathing problems. Those who live in rural areas have other problems, such as "farmer's lung" or pesticides that are poured onto the land.

I remember hearing about a case where a farmer's wife went into the field to take the farmer his lunch, and found him sitting on his tractor in a state of confusion, Apparently, this had been caused by something inhaled - perhaps from the tractor's exhaust - or some pesticide absorbed through his skin. because he'd forgotten how to drive the tractor. There is also the story of a lady who suffered asbestos damage to her lungs just by washing her husband's overalls. The husband was a dock worker who worked on naval ships. Why did she get ill and not him? I believe it is down to the individual's immune system, and while some people have more resistance to illness, it may be that the sufferer was not in the best of health and strength at the time, and thus vulnerable to going down with something.

Eating and drinking sensibly, and avoiding smoking will result in better health, but I also wonder if the increase in the number of people with memory loss could be a result of years of eating food contaminated with chemicals? Perhaps the length of time spent by the younger generation using mobile phones may result in an outbreak of brain tumours in the future.

Anger, Worry and Stress

One of the biggest causes of ill health is Stress, and the main contributions to Stress are Anger and Worry.

Anger + Worry = Stress = Illness

When we worry we get depressed. We might choose to go to the doctor and we might be prescribed antidepressant drugs. It can become hard for someone to live in the real world if he or she takes such drugs for too long, but Energy Healing and meditation can break the negative habit of worry. Some people are natural worriers who worry even when they have nothing to worry about, but in reality, there are only two days that you can do nothing about – one being yesterday and the other being tomorrow.

To live we need food, clothing and shelter, so anything else is a bonus, but perhaps we have come to expect too much, and maybe we forget what we already have.

While the physical illness is easy to see, the psychological ailments that people suffer from are less evident. These illnesses can result in depression, anxiety and isolation. When we are children, the first seven years of life is when we need the support of our parents and extended family, and above all, we need to know we are wanted, loved and protected. However, this doesn't always happen, and If there is a historical reason for a person's depression, Energy Healing will help break the cycle.

Preparing to Heal

We have looked at the mechanics of the healing energy, and now we need to put it into practice. The success of healing depends on a combination of different things, the first of which is the way the healer controls and delivers the flow of healing energy.

Before we can heal others we must first heal ourselves. Just as we get the best light from a torch with fully charged batteries, it is the same for the healer, because when we are healthy in mind, body and spirit, we are at our optimum strength for healing others. So the first thing we need to do is give ourselves regular self-healing. I have known people who completed a Reiki course and rushed out to give healing to everyone who needs it; but after a Reiki attunement, there is always a three week cleansing period where the Chakras are cleared of any negative vibrations, and it is unwise to try to heal until this period is complete.

The best place to start working on yourself is somewhere where you won't be disturbed. The light should be dim and some relaxing instrumental music will help. You need to sensitise your hands by rubbing the palms together. Then put your hands in the prayer position in front of your heart saying to yourself, *"It is my intention to carry out self-healing on myself. I ask my guardian angel and my healing guides to assist with this healing"*. The important part is the intention, because everything in the universe starts with a thought, and the mind generates the thought and sends the message to the body.

Start your self-healing by grounding yourself in this way:

• Imagine roots coming out of the soles of your feet and making their way through the various layers of earth until they connect with the crystal at the centre of the planet.

• Now open your Crown Chakra by imaging it as a large lotus flower with the petals unfolding. Visualise the light / divine energy coming down from the cosmos through the Crown Chakra, past the Third Eye (brow Chakra), the Throat Chakra and entering the Heart Chakra.

• From here the energy flows down your arms and into the palms of your hands, so now you should feel the heat starting to build in your palms.

Taking Things Further
• Start the self-healing at your head by placing your palms on either side of it, but keep your palms about half an inch away from your head. It won't be long before you feel the energy flowing from your palms.

• Stay in this position for five minutes before moving to the Third Eye.

• Each Chakra should be given five minutes of healing, so after the Third Eye, move to the throat, heart, Solar plexus, Sacral and finally the Base Chakra.

If your hands are in any one position for five minutes and the flow of energy is still strong (this is indicated by the heat from your palms), you can remain there longer. However, if you need to move to the next position, you must remove your hands slowly, in order to avoid a sudden disruption to the flow of energy.

If you are in a public place, you can still give yourself healing by saying the intention in your mind. You can also still put your hands onto your own person – say by putting your hands on your lap - because the healing will flow onwards from that point to the place in which it happens to be needed.

When you have finished self-healing, it is important to give thanks to your guardian angel and healing guides.

Pauline's Client

Pauline, who is a healer, had a client who was suffering from a frozen shoulder, but during the healing Pauline noticed the energy was flowing to the man's solar plexus area. On completion of the healing session she mentioned this to the gentleman, and suggested he should go and see a doctor to have a check-up. He did as she suggested and as a result, he was diagnosed with the early stages of pancreatic cancer. Two years later, he returned to see Pauline; he told her the cancer had gone and he asked if she could now sort out his frozen shoulder!

Useful Notes for Beginners

Being new to healing, you may not actually feel the energy flowing, but have faith in what you are doing because it still works, even though you can't feel anything happening.

- The more you practise, the stronger your healing ability becomes.
- Some people feel cold instead of heat in the palms of their hands.

Location and Ambience
When you give healing, the ambiance of the location is again important, as follows:

- Ideally the room should be kept solely for the purpose of healing, but that isn't always possible.
- The room should be warm but not hot.
- A low light is best.
- Freshen the room by opening a window before the client arrives.
- If you like, you can burn white sage incense sticks to cleanse the room, but avoid burning incense during the healing because the patient may have breathing problems.
- Soft gentle music will help you and the patient relax.
- You can give healing with the patient lying on a couch or sitting in a chair.
- If they are lying on a couch they only need to remove their spectacles and shoes.
- It is a good idea to place a blanket over them before you start the Energy Healing.

> *One lady used to give healing in her home, but it was never successful. The failure might have had something to do with her dog, which barked all the time.*

MAKING A START

Before you start the healing, state your intention to heal (state the name of the patient), and then ask your guardian angel and healing guides and your patient's guardian angel and healing guides to assist in the healing. Now you should follow the same routine as you did with the self-healing, only this time on the patient. Remember it is not necessary to touch the patient, but you have to be comfortable and to avoid straining yourself in an effort to keep your hands hovering above the body. It is all right to lay your hands gently on the patient, but avoid contact with the female breasts and male and female genital areas. If you are healing children, always ensure that the parent or guardian is present. There is no need for the patient to remove any clothing except for shoes and spectacles.

> *I am sometimes fortunate to have a female healing assistant who works with me when I give healing, and this means the patient gets healing energy from two people.*

Working on the Patient

As with self-healing, you should spend at least five minutes on each of the Chakras, starting with the Crown Chakra. After you have worked down to the Base Chakra, you should move down to the knees and then the feet. When I get to the feet, I stand at the base of the bed and gently place my hands on the patient's feet. If my assistant is with me, she places her hands on each side of the patient's head. I visualise dragging any negative energy down the body through my arms down my legs and letting it fall away down through the floor. At the same time my assistant at the head is pushing cosmic energy down through the patient's body. You would be surprised how many people actually feel the energy flowing down through their bodies.

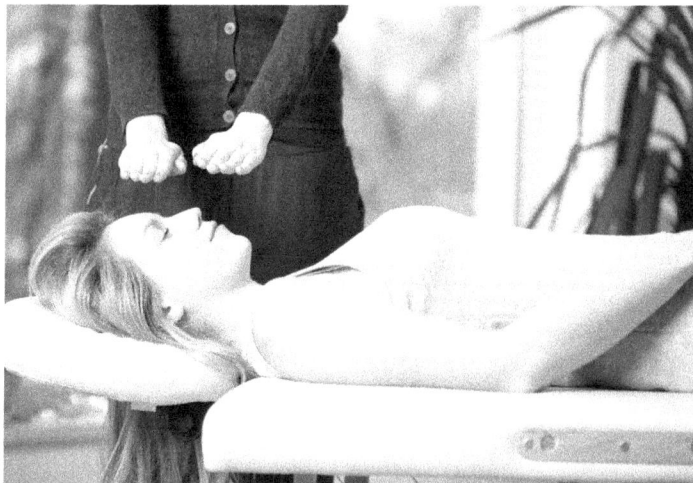

Completing the Healing

On completion of the healing, you should give thanks to the spiritual beings that have helped you to carry out the healing. Break the healing connection with a cutting motion with your arms and hands in front of your body, while at the same time stepping back as this breaks the connection between you and your patient. Now wash your hands to remove any residual negative energy. Tell the patient that they should drink plenty of water during the day and also tell them that the healing will carry on inside their bodies for weeks after receiving the Energy Healing. Ensure that your patient is back in the real world and fully grounded before he or she leaves.

Six: Distant Healing

Energy Healing in Focus

One Wednesday morning while I was at my weekly Tai-Chi class, I suddenly felt my energy flow to my friend Angie who was standing next to me. After the lesson had ended, Angie, who is also a Reiki healer, told me that at the time that I felt the flow of energy, she was sending distant healing to her brother-in-law, Micky, who at that precise moment was attending a funeral. Because Angie and I work together as healers, when she opened up, my energy automatically linked with hers. That evening, Angie rang her sister to find out how the funeral went. Her sister told Angie that it went well, but that at one point during the service Micky had to take his jacket off because he was too hot!

The mind is an effective tool, and in the church that I attend, we have a prayer tree with the names of those who need healing written on paper leaves which we hang from the tree, because the combined prayers of the congregation are a powerful force. For instance, a lady in Germany who had cancer with little chance of survival, was named on our prayer tree. She not only survived, but when she was better, she travelled to Plymouth and during the Sunday service, she went to the healing tree and removed the leaf that had her name on it, saying that she no longer needed the help. She also thanked us all for our prayers.

Faith and Distant Healing

I believe that distant healing is sometimes more powerful then hands on healing. An example of this is Jesus, who

6: Distant Healing

was a great healer. He used distant healing when he cured the centurion's servant who had been in pain, paralyzed and near death. Divine or spiritual healing isn't confined to Christianity, as it is common to all religions, and even to shamanism.

Lourdes in the south west region of France has become one of the world's leading Catholic shrines, and it is well known for its pilgrimages and miracles. The small town with a population of 15,000 people is boosted by 5,000,000 pilgrims every season (March - October). People go there to pray on behalf of loved ones who are ill, and those who are in poor health themselves also make the pilgrimage.

In England, Harry Edwards (1893 – 1976) was one of the most renowned of the more recent healers, and he used to receive between 9,000 and 11,000 letters a week requesting distant healing. On one occasion he even gave a public demonstration of healing in front of 6,000 people at the Royal Albert Hall.

Today there is a healing sanctuary that carries on the work of Harry Edwards, and this sanctuary still receives requests for distant healing in addition to offering contact healing to those who can attend in person. It's a fact that the combined energy of people who come together for a similar purpose is very strong, as we see at times during a sports match or a pop concert.

Many years ago, my friend, Tania, knew nothing about Energy Healing until she came across it through her then mother-in-law, Muriel. The old lady suffered terribly with osteoarthritis and rheumatoid arthritis, and this often made her very bad tempered. Muriel's son and daughter were good to her, as was Tania herself, but it was often a thankless task due to the old girl's unpleasant outbursts.

Despite her bad nature, Muriel had a couple of friends who took pity on her, and they made a point of taking her to the Wimbledon healing centre to receive healing from Harry Edwards and others who worked their magic in that place. After a few weeks, the inflammatory flare-ups that plagued Muriel eased, and within a few months they stopped altogether. While her twisted bones did not miraculously straighten out again, they did stop hurting her.

Over time, Muriel's nature mellowed, and she began to open up to Tania about her difficult youth and the harrowing events of her early life. Among other things, she told Tania about the pain she'd felt after the dreadful loss of her eldest child, Derek, who had died at the age of four from bacterial meningitis. This of course had happened long before the age of antibiotics, but even now this is a dangerous illness for a small child. Several years later, Muriel told Tania that she could feel the little boy around her, and it was no surprise to Tania to hear a few days later that the old lady had died from a stroke.

Muriel's life should have been easy in her later years, but it was marred by the pain of her arthritis, and when Harry Edwards and his friends stepped in, they made her life bearable. This impressed Tania, but not as much as the change that the healing worked on the old lady's nature; slowly but surely, Muriel changed from crabby, foul tempered, secretive and untrusting, to open, cheerful and thoughtful. It was like watching the effects of a slow-acting magic spell.

6: Distant Healing

If Tania ever needed proof that healing works, that was it, but Tania saw straight away that those who believe that one trip to a healer is enough to cure anything are wrong. The improvement in Muriel's health and temper was amazing, but it took two whole years before its effects became complete.

How to Send Distant Healing

When we send distant healing, we first need to connect with that person. Just as with hands-on healing, the energy will flow from the healer's aura to that of the patient, and this is also when our thoughts of love and compassion come into the equation, as they boost the effect for the patient who receives the healing. The work happens on a mental level, and we use our higher selves to send the healing to the recipient's higher self, from where it is then directed to the patient's mind and body. There are bound to be examples of this effect in your own life when you consider the times that you have found yourself thinking about someone, and then they contact you. Just like telepathy, healing can be sent over great distances, because in reality we are all connected.

The ideal way to send distant healing is by arranging a time between the sender and the receiver of the healing. Then the person receiving the healing can relax and be open for the healing energy. Just like hands on healing, the healer should "put in the intention" of sending the healing, and ask help from above to facilitate the healing. Then the healer will connect with his higher self and healing guides, asking them to send the healing to the patient's higher self and the patient's healing guides. It is helpful for the healer to imagine the person receiving the healing energy by having the image of the person in mind, and for this a photograph might be helpful. Some people use a cuddly toy or pillow as a substitute for the person being healed, using the hands-on method on the surrogate object to carry out the healing. The cuddly toy or pillow is only a means of focusing the healing energy, but even so you would be surprised how hot the palms of the hands get as you send the healing energy. Never use a real person or animal as a substitute for distant healing. Distant healing should not take as long as the hands-on method does, so fifteen to twenty minutes is about the right time. On completion of healing, it is important to give thanks and detach yourself from the healing.

> *Prayer is another form of distant healing*

I am sometimes asked if it is necessary for the person receiving to know that they are being sent healing. We don't heal to gratify our ego, we do it to help others, so if you think the person you want to send healing to might be offended or not want the healing, you can send the healing to that person's higher self, and it will be their choice to accept the healing or not. All we can do is send the healing from a pure heart with love and compassion. Remember we all have free will and the healing energy accepts that, although amazingly, some people don't want to be healed - and we will look at why this happens later in this book.

Similarly, when you send distant healing to someone in a coma or who is suffering from Alzheimer's or Dementia, it is their higher self that will accept the healing. While on the subject of consent, I have on occasions been asked to give healing to animals. Needless to say, the dog or cat did not ask for the healing, but they were very grateful all the same. Dogs are lazy, so given the chance, they would stay there all day soaking up the energy. Cats on the other hand, will jump off your lap or table when they have had enough. If you are in a position to give Energy Healing to a horse, then be sure you switch your healing on before you go near the horse and always approach the animal from the front, because horses are very sensitive to human energy.

Animals love healing energy, because they know it is given with love and compassion. For me, it is sometimes easier to understand those who have more time for their pets than they do for their fellow man.

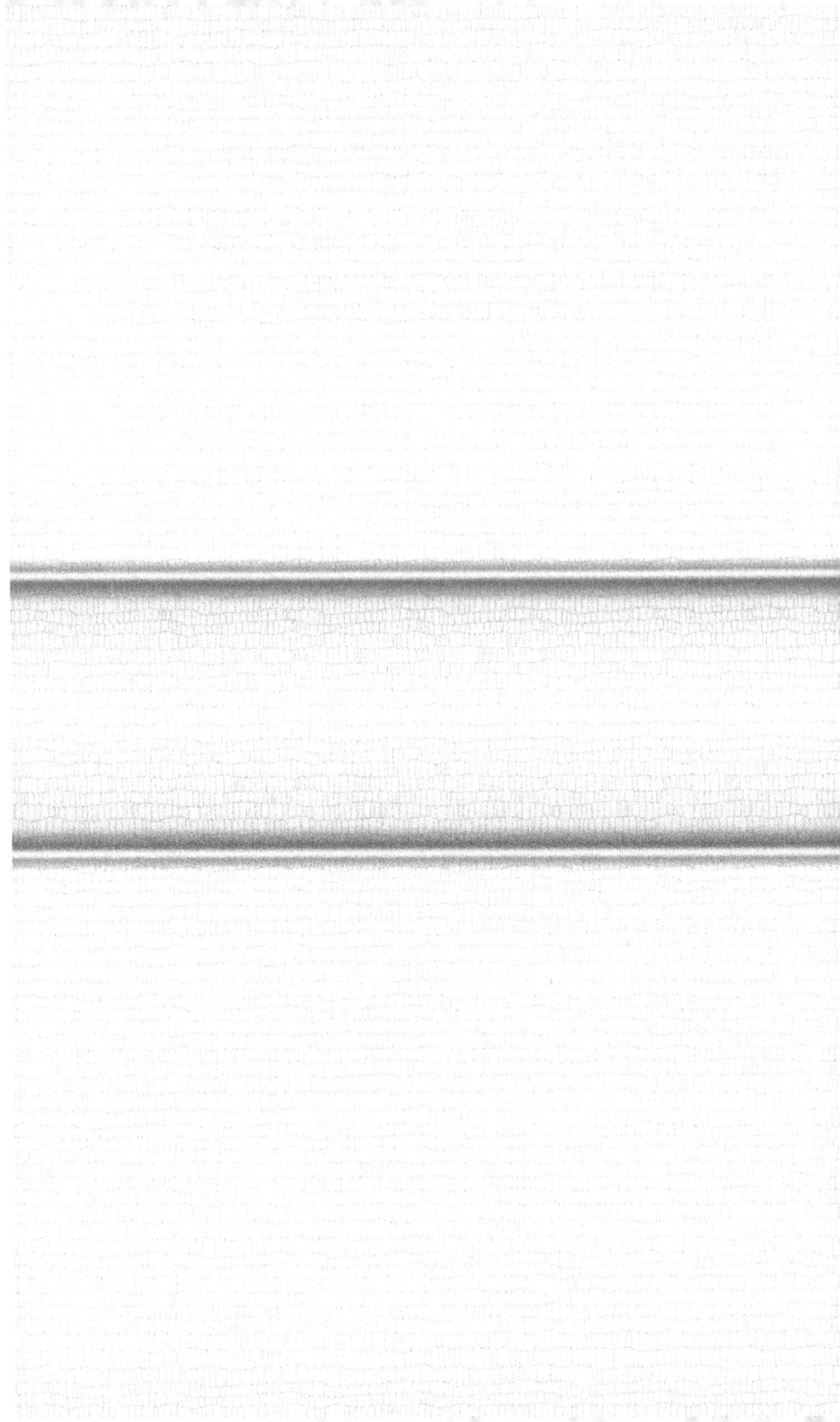

Seven:
Meditation and Visualisation

Meditation

Meditation is a central part of several religions but it can also be practised by non-believers. By using meditation, we clear our minds of unwanted thoughts and worries, thus allowing ourselves to achieve self-awareness. There are many different methods of meditation - for instance, Christian meditation includes quietly praying or just contemplating the love of Christ for oneself and for mankind.

Different people use various techniques to meditate. Some chant, which leads to a hypnotic state that clears the mind, while others play music and burn incense. Don't play music with lyrics; perhaps treat yourself to one of the many CDs that will help you chill out. Having said this, you don't need to sit in the lotus position and chant mantras or even play music, because you can ·simply sit upright in a comfortable chair in a quiet place, and clear your mind of all thoughts for half an hour. That should do the trick. When you start to meditate, you might find it hard to clear your mind, but there are many ways to achieve this. For instance, take three deep breaths, while concentrating in turn on the in breaths and then the out breaths.

If we wish to fill ourselves with universal love, we first have to empty the cup. Once we clear our minds, we can start to put the positive and healing thoughts in, so there are affirmations we can repeat. For example, you could say:

7: Meditation & Visualisation

"My real self is happy and perfect,

and illness is an illusion".

"I Am Light: I Am Love".

Repeat these phrases to yourself several times and believe the message, because it is true.

The Power of Thought and Visualization

Visualization is also a powerful tool for healing. The root of stress is in our minds, because we create anger and worry through negative thoughts. Don't underestimate the power of your thoughts - they can be used to heal as well as to harm. We tend to use our intellect far more than our imagination or intuition.

Visualization in meditation can bring about this communication with your real self (soul / spirit), so in this way, by using our imagination, we are sending a message to our subconscious. The old adage, "be careful what you wish for" is very true. When we visualize, we must be clear about what we want. And it should not be used to harm others. You may want a better job or you may want the ideal partner, but it is important you don't put faces to the partner or friend whom you want to attract. Your "higher self" knows what is right for you. If you are ill, you should visualize yourself becoming closer to your "real self", which is perfect and free from sickness and pain.

Ancient Wisdom

In the esoteric traditions of the Far East, there is a belief that our physical world is an illusion behind which exists a "Greater Reality", but we in the West only accept what we can touch, taste, see or smell. We need to realise that there is no solid matter! It is only energy moving at such a low frequency that gives it the illusion of form. When we accept that there are worlds existing at subatomic levels where our spirit or soul has its reality, this is where the Power of Thought and Visualization are supreme. As we said before, the real you (soul / spirit / higher self) is perfect and free from illness. We are spirit, although while on earth we also have a physical presence. Our body in this life is like the clothes that we put on in the morning, but at the end of the day (when we die) we discard these clothes. The next day we are reborn (rein-carnated) so we put on different cloths, but as spirit we remain the same. Some of the lessons that we learn in this life are carried over with us to the next life, and we keep coming back through a number of lives until we reach the stage of perfection, and after that there is no need for us to "get dressed" (reincarnated), because we can then stay in the realm of perfection.

Eight:
Healing the Past and the Future

Energy Healing in Focus

Pain in the Past

Once we accept that Energy Healing works, it opens more diverse ways of using our healing. For example, healing the past is important if we are to be free and allow ourselves to live to our full potential of a happy and healthy life. Some past issues can be buried so deeply that we don't admit to ourselves that they exist, and childhood trauma can be both physical and mental. As children we depend on our parents and those in positions of authority to protect and love us. Whey they let us down, it leaves a wound that remains open, and we carry this pain through our lives like a heavy weight within our being.

There can be many causes for these past wounds. For instance, children who lose a parent at an early age may feel they are being punished, so self-blame is a common symptom of these historical events. It is important to bring the cause into the open and accept that it needs to be healed, and then we can send healing back to the time when the problem arose. You might ask how we can send healing to a time and an event that has already happened, maybe long ago. Well, the following story might help you to understand this.

There is an acquaintance of mine who I will call Ruth. Ruth's mother was a German lady who came to London with her British husband at a time when it was not uncommon for British serviceman to marry local girls while they were stationed in Germany. When Ruth's

8: Healing the Past and the Future

mother came to London, she had no friends and she spoke no English, so she learned to speak the language by listening to BBC radio.

When Ruth was a child, her father used to lock her in the bedroom while he would mercilessly beat her mother and the sound of her mother suffering had a lasting effect on Ruth. Ruth's father was also a womaniser and he drank to excess. Ruth and her mother never forgave her father for his brutish behaviour and whenever Ruth went to see a medium and her father came through, she could not and would not forgive him. At the present time while I am writing this, Ruth's ability to forgive is still a work in progress. Healing the past does not change what happened, but it can allow forgiveness and healing to permeate back into that time.

Healing the Past
It is easier if we look at the past, present and future as three lines running alongside each other in parallel rather than linear form, as this makes it much easier to access the past by jumping from one line to another, rather than travelling back in time.

If possible, dig out a photograph of whoever requires the healing from a time close to the date that requires healing. If you don't have a photograph, then write down what happened and the date on a piece of paper (the paper can be burnt later). Visualise the event and send healing in the same way that you do for distant healing. The photograph or written account is nothing to do with witchcraft or voodoo; it is merely a tool that will focus the mind.

Energy Healing in Focus

We can also carry things that require healing from past lives or previous reincarnations. A friend of mine had a recurring dream of being crucified. This always started with her looking up at a star filled sky, and then while she was on the cross, a Roman centurion would break her legs with a metal bar. In her present life she complained of having pains in her lower legs, which she put down to the fact that she did a lot of horse riding, but the pains could have been caused or exacerbated by the past life experience of having her legs deliberately smashed.

We associate crucifixion as being nailed to a cross, but this was not always the case; sometimes the person being executed would be attached to the cross with ropes, and a footrest placed below the feet for the purpose of taking the person's weight off their wrists. Sometimes this footrest can be seen in representations of the crucifixion of Jesus. It was a tradition to break the legs of the person being crucified when they were hung on the cross to prevent them being untied and escaping.

The typical crucifixion lasted several days, with the person raising himself up to breathe and then slumping back down again, owing to the effort this required and the pain it caused. When the person slumped back down, he struggled to breathe and as his strength ran out he slowly suffocated. Needless to say, thirst also played a part, although not hunger, because we tend not to feel hunger when in severe pain and distress.

The way to heal this kind of trauma from a past life is to forgive those who did us harm and also to ask for forgiveness for the wrongs we may have done others during our own previous lifetimes.

8: Healing the Past and the Future

Healing the Future

We all have to cope with things that we are not looking forward to, and it could be something as mundane as a driving test or some other stressful event. However, we might also like to send healing to the time when we come to die, thus enabling us and our loved ones to cope more easily with our transition to the next life.

On a more immediate note, if someone is going to have an operation in the future, then it would be good to send healing to that future date. When we send healing to the future it is similar to sending it to the past, in that it may not change things but it will allow us to handle the situation more easily.

Why Healing Doesn't Always Work

If you ask someone who is ill, "Do you really want to be healed?" they will most likely say, "Yes I of course I want to be healed". But how many times do you see hospital patients in their dressing gowns standing outside the hospital entrance, connected to their life saving equipment, smoking a cigarette? I have even seen a pregnant woman smoking a cigarette outside the maternity department. They have been told that smoking is bad for them but they still carry on, and the same goes for the alcoholic with a liver transplant who continues to drink. I am sure that they believe that they want to live a healthy life, but they have subconsciously become attached to their addictions and they have grown to accept the ailments that arise from them. Strange though it may seem, some people are nervous of the responsibility that will come with perfect health.

Energy Healing in Focus

As a healer I have come across people who are afraid to be healed. Our society, with its free and available health care and disability support systems can subconsciously be an obstacle for some who want to change. This doesn't mean we should scrap disability payments to people and their families who rely on them, but in some cases, the continued illness might be a way of saving the person from having to face reality or to strive and struggle in the way that healthy people do. Hanging on to sickness can also be a way of attracting affection from our loved ones. All of these reasons may be in the subconscious.

When we visit the doctor, we feel cheated if we don't come away with a prescription for some form of medication, and to some extent, we have become a nation of hypochondriacs. A survey in England in 2013 showed that fifty per cent of the adult population take regular prescription drugs, with cholesterol-lowering statins, pain relief and anti-depressants being among the most prescribed drugs. The cost to the NHS was £15 billion per annum in that year – and that is just for England.

8: Healing the Past and the Future

Conventional medicine usually only treats the symptoms of the illness. Do you want to be reliant on the large pharmaceutical companies for your future well-being? The Holistic approach, which includes Energy Healing, treats the cause of illness in the body, mind and soul. In ancient China, the village doctor was paid to prevent illness, so if none of the inhabitants of his village became ill, he was doing his job well but if too many people got sick, he was sacked!

How would you feel if your doctor told you to rest, stop eating for twenty-four hours and drink plenty of water? We lose our appetites when we fall ill, and this is a message from our bodies telling us to give our digestive systems a chance to rest. Our body uses energy to turn the food we eat into fuel to sustain life, but by resting the process of digestion, this energy can be redirected to help with our inbuilt natural healing abilities. We are equipped with amazing and sophisticated healing processes that allow our bodies to repair and maintain themselves, as long as we allow them to do so. New research has shown that ninety-eight per cent of the cells in our body are renewed each year, which means that the liver gradually replaces itself every six weeks, while skin is renewed every month and the stomach lining every four days. Many things have an effect on this natural regeneration, but it helps if we eat a healthy balanced diet and drink plenty of water. We also need to get enough sleep and avoid stress where possible.

The process of healing needs the consent of the person who is ill before the healing can take effect, so it may be a good idea to ask the patient if they really want to be healed, before carrying out Energy Healing.

Nine: Eastern Influences

Tai-Chi and Qi Gong

When it comes to Energy Healing, the people from the eastern hemisphere are miles ahead of us. A large number of hospitals in China have officially adopted Qi Gong as one method for treating cancer, arthritis, and many other medical conditions. Indeed, they are returning to traditional methods of healing with surprisingly good results.

The old Chinese philosophy believes the chi (energy) that is within us falls into two categories, these being pre-natal and post-natal. The pre-natal chi is supplied by the parents at the time of conception. The man will provide the Yang energy for the baby and the women supplies the Yin energy. The more harmonious the relationship between the mother and father, the healthier will be their offspring. The health of the parents will also be a factor in the pre-natal chi, so if the parents live a healthy life style, eating properly and avoiding harmful drugs, alcohol and smoking, the chances are that the baby will be born with good health. The male up to the point of conception needs to have maintained a healthy lifestyle because as the old saying goes, "Poor seeds don't grow good crops".

After conception, the mother supplies the chi through the umbilical cord, and it isn't just nutritional support that the baby needs, he also needs to know he is wanted and loved by all around him. The unborn baby can sense these things while still in the womb. The mental state of the mother is just as important to the unborn child, as she also needs to know that she will have the necessary love and support when the child is born.

The post-natal chi is supplied by and through the people and environment the baby is born into. If a baby is born to a single mother whose partner or husband has left her, she may feel resentment towards the baby. This could result in the child having a low level of chi, leading to the child being susceptible to sickness and perhaps also of behavioural issues. However, we mustn't despair if the conditions are not right when the child is born, because even the weakest plant can become strong with the right care and attention, as is often the case with children who are adopted or cared for by relatives other than the natural parents.

A healthy person has an abundance of internal energy flowing through their body, nourishing their internal organs. This builds a strong immunity against diseases.

The Chinese have a strong family tradition, so they tend to look after their parents when they get old. The Chinese also maintain a more active lifestyle than we do. I remember when a Chinese man was being interviewed after running a marathon at the age of a hundred, he said, "I only took up marathon running at the age of ninety after my wife died."

The energy within the body does not remain stagnant and there are two primary channels that carry a strong flow of energy through the body. One of these channels is called "The Functional Channel". This starts at the perineum, which is a point between the genital area and the anus. This energy flows upwards past the genitals, stomach organs, heart and throat.

The second channel, called "The Governor Channel", starts from the same point at the perineum, but flows up the back of the body through the coccyx or tail bone, through the spine, into the brain and then over the front of the skull, to end at the roof of the mouth. The tongue can be used to connect these two primary channels of energy, so when we press the tip of our tongue to the roof of the mouth (you are trying it now, aren't you?) we get a continuous flow of energy that goes up the back of the body through the spine and down the front. The Chinese call this "The Small Heavenly Cycle" or "The Microcosmic Orbit". Remember the energy flows up the front and up the back before the Microcosmic Orbit is linked by pressing the tip of your tongue against the roof of your mouth.

The Functional Channel which travels up the front of the body has a Yin or cold nature, and the Governor Channel, up the back has a Yang or hot nature. When our Base or root Chakra is open, we receive the Yin cold energy from the Earth and when our Crown Chakra is open, we receive the Yang warm energy from the sun and beyond. When The Microcosmic Orbit is linked, the Yin and Yang energy mix to become a warm energy. It is not necessary to spend our days going around with our tongues pressed against the roofs of our mouths, because when we meditate, our energy tends to flow up to our brain. We may feel hot while meditating, which is why it is important to be grounded by connecting to the earth before we meditate.

9: Eastern Influences

By using the mind and will-power, it is possible with practice to focus your energy in one place, on or in your body. Martial arts masters can focus their energy to their Tan-Tien - this is the area above and below the belly button, which they connect to the earth. There are various film clips on youtube.com demonstrating this technique, and showing how four strong men cannot lift or move one man when he uses this energy to connect himself to the earth. A simple example of this is if you ever tried to put a child into a push chair when they didn't want to get into it – the child somehow manages to turn his body into a plank of wood!

> *If you want to know more about gaining mastery over your body's energy system, try the book "Awaken Healing Energy Through the Tao" by Mantak Chia.*

According to the Mayo Clinic, more than 2.5 million Americans now practice Tai-Chi to reduce stress and anxiety, increase energy, stamina and flexibility, muscle strength and balance. There is also evidence that Tai-Chi improves immune response, sleeping patterns, lowers cholesterol levels, relieves joint pain, and in older people reduces the risk of falls by improving balance.

Although similar, Tai-Chi is a form of martial arts whereas Qi-Gong is considered a health system. Qi-Gong is part of the Chinese National Health Plan and it is practised in schools, universities and hospitals. You can practise the arts of Qi-Gong and Tai-Chi on your own, but when practised in a group, it has the benefit of a combined energy force. It is even better when you practise in the open air, among trees or by the sea.

Shiatsu

Up to this point, we have only talked about using energy to heal, and the closest that we came to massage was the gentle laying on of hands. We know that if we are in pain or suffer an injury, the self-healing instinct in us encourages us to put our hands over the area of pain and massage it. Shiatsu literally means finger (Shi) pressure (atsu). Shiatsu works by stimulating the body with the palm of the hand, fingers and thumbs. There is also a barefoot Shiatsu where the healers use their feet as well as their hands to massage the patient.

It is believed that a Japanese boy called Tokujiro Namikoshi discovered Shiatsu in 1912. When Tokujiro was only seven, he cured his mother of rheumatism by using his fingers, thumbs and palms to apply pressure. As he grew up, he studied anatomy and physiology, and in 1957, Shiatsu was accepted by the Japanese Medical Ministry of Welfare as a recognised form of healing. In

9: Eastern Influences

February 1954, while on honeymoon with Joe Di Maggio, Marilyn Monroe was treated by Tokujiro Namikoshi for insomnia and the treatment was a success, which helped Shiatsu to become known around the world. While visiting the USA in 1973, Tokujiro Namikoshi treated Mohammad Ali while he was training for a fight.

As with other forms of Energy Healing, it is important that the Shiatsu practitioner must be in a good state of health, as he or she will need strength or he will tire too easily. Shiatsu won't feel good and it won't work if the person giving it is ailing in mind or body. Because Shiatsu requires coordination between the mind and body, the healer's thinking needs to be clear and precise. The person giving the Shiatsu normally wears loose fitting clothes made from natural fibres, as this helps with the flow of energy. The patient lies on a futon on the floor. *(A futon is a quilted Japanese mattress.)*

The Shiatsu practitioner is trained to observe the patient at the first meeting, as a visual diagnosis can tell a lot about a person, and indeed, the following psychological traits reflect possible internal problems:

- A patient showing signs of fear = kidneys problems.
- Serious timidity = lung problems.
- Laughing excessively = heart problems.
- Anger or short temper = liver problems
- Moodiness = stomach problems.

The colour of the skin is a good indication of a person's health. For example, you will notice the skin of a heavy smoker tends to be grey and lifeless. The posture of the patient is also an indicator, because someone who stands with the upper part of the body leaning forward with the lower abdomen protruding may suffer from a weak digestive system. Someone with an extremely expanded abdomen suggests constipation and flatulence, and they may also suffer from back problems. As well as the massage, the practitioner uses his or her intuition to note the symptoms and causes of the illness, as this will assist with the healing.

There is an amount of pressure used in the massage upon the patient, which means that Shiatsu should not be given to people with serious illnesses such as heart conditions, multiple sclerosis or cancer. Care must be taken with pregnant women, and certain body areas should be avoided.

Reflexology
Reflexology is another hands-on traditional Chinese healing technique but this also has links with other Eastern cultures, such as those in Egypt. Reflexology uses specific points and energy zones on the feet, hands, scalp and ears to treat the muscles and organs of the body. When pain is felt in one part of the body - for example, in the sciatic nerve - massaging a point on the sole of the foot below the heel can relieve it.

Reflexology practitioners work mainly on the feet, although other areas of massage can also be beneficial. Our hands have an electrical field; the right hand gives out positive (Yang) energy and the left hand gives out negative (Yin) energy. When the practitioner uses the right hand, he or she stimulates the nerve endings with positive (Yang) energy, so this would be used to clear a blockage and revitalise the body. If a calming effect is

9: Eastern Influences

required in order to control pain, then the left hand negative (Yin) energy is used.

The reflexology massage should be given in a calm and relaxed environment and in a room that is quiet and warm. The patient receiving the healing should feel comfortable, so he or she should lie on a bed or sit in a special reclining chair that supports the back. When the patient's shoes and socks are removed the feet can be cleaned with warm water or a hot damp towel. As well as cleaning the feet for hygiene purposes, this will help to make the skin soft and supple.

At the start, both feet are massaged at the same time, but when the main part of the treatment starts, the right foot is treated first. It is believed that the right foot is linked to our past, so any past emotions can be dealt with first, before moving to the left foot, which represents the present and future. The actual massage should feel gentle and enjoyable, and as with all forms of healing, it is important that the person giving the healing is professionally trained, qualified and insured.

Acupuncture

Acupuncture is another traditional form of Chinese healing, and it can be used for various things from stopping smoking to pain relief. Like Shiatsu and reflexology, acupuncture is safe when carried out by a trained practitioner who only uses clean needles. Unlike other forms of Energy Healing, it is the skill and knowledge of the acupuncturist that is important rather than the healer's energy.

The body comprises two natural forces called Yin and Yang. Yin is the female energy which is cool, calm and passive, while Yang is the male force which is stimulating, hot and aggressive. We all have both these forces within us, and when there is an imbalance between our Yin and Yang this leads to illness and disease. An excess of Yang energy can result in headaches and hypertension, and too much Yin energy can cause tiredness, feeling cold and being lethargic. Acupuncture will establish whether there is an imbalance between the Yin and Yang, and use needles to rectify the problems.

As we saw earlier in this book, meridians are the channels through which the energy flows. Imagine these meridians as energy motorways, and there are also "A" roads and "B" roads.

There are twelve major meridians which connect to the major organs, including the stomach, bladder, kidneys and liver, while secondary meridians are sometimes referred to as "vessels". Along the meridians there are what are called acupoints; these are entrances to the meridians, and within these 500 acupoints are what are called "the ten golden points", which deal with the major organs. These are where the acupuncturist inserts the needles in order to clear the energy flow. Acupoints are located all over the body. For instance, the acupoints for the large intestine can be found in the arm above the elbow, and the kidney meridian can be found in the upper part of the leg. Remember, these are like motor-ways and we can access them along the route.

Acupuncture has been around for centuries for relief of pain and it can even be used for anaesthesia prior to surgery or childbirth, because certain sites located within the body produce endorphins which increase the resis-tance to pain. A natural form of morphine exists within our bodies, and by using acupuncture, this can be released.

Used in conjunction with acupuncture needles, there is a technique called cupping. Cotton wool is placed inside glass cups or jars, and these are used by inverting them and placing them on a particular meridian line. The cotton wool is burnt, creating a vacuum in the jar, which has the effect of drawing energy to the cup, and then needles are used to stimulate the healing energy.

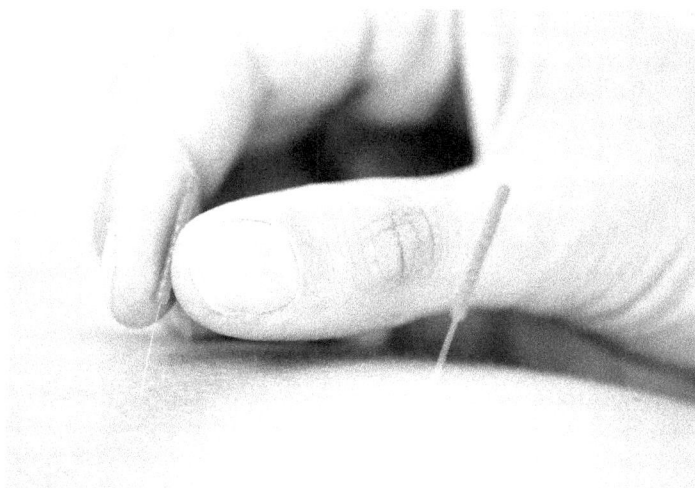

Energy Healing in Focus

A similar type of treatment is Electro-acupuncture, which was first used in China in 1934. The treatment involves the use of small electric currents being passed through two needles. The advantage of this method is that it provides a steady flow of electrical pulses, and the intensity and frequency of these pulses can be adjusted.

Ten: Crystal Healing

The use of crystals in healing is growing and this is witnessed by the popularity of shops that sell them. A shop in Plymouth called "Phoenix Wings Crystals" started with a small stall in the market, but because of the demand, the family have now moved to a bigger shop on the high street. If you attend any of the numerous Mind, Body and Spirit fairs, you will see a number of stalls selling crystals, and the beauty of it is that you can buy some crystals for just a pound. There is also a large amount of literature detailing the use of the various crystals, and perhaps the best known book is "The Crystal Bible" by Judy Hall, which features over 200 crystals.

Crystals can be divided into two categories, namely precious stones and semi-precious stones. In the precious category you have the girl's best friend, diamonds, as well as rubies, emeralds, and sapphires. Among the semi-precious crystals - also called gemstones - you have carnelians, garnets, rock crystals and lapis lazuli. These were used for ornamentation as well as symbols of power; they were valued by ancient peoples for the secret meanings that they carried. A polished stone is pretty to look at, while unpolished stones in their raw state might not look as attractive, but their healing power is identical.

Other than Tektite, which is a meteorite from an extra-terrestrial origin, crystals come from within the earth and they are the result of an inhospitable environment that involves high temperatures and pressures. Deep beneath our feet, the earth is in constant turmoil, which can be seen by volcanic eruptions and earthquakes that appear on the surface. The cycle of a crystal formation involves it being pushed up, eroded, transported and compressed, which manifests in a complete change of form, structure, substance, character and appearance, and it can take millions of years for a crystal to work its way to the surface. It is the different minerals from which a crystal originates that make it what it eventually becomes.

Crystals such as quartz come from the fiery gases and molten minerals that are found deep within the earth, and they cool and solidify as they make their way to the surface. The slow process of change sometimes creates a bubble of gas within the earth and it is here that a crystal can grow. The value of the crystal is judged by its purity and rarity, which is why diamonds are so expensive.

Diamonds are used to cleanse the aura, and they are also useful on a spiritual level, as they activate the Crown Chakra which links us to the Divine Light. Industrial or synthetic diamonds are produced in an artificial process, but they are made from the same materials as natural diamonds, such as pure carbon, crystallized by using high pressure, high temperatures and a chemical vapour deposition. Because of their hardness, these diamonds are used as an abrasive in grinding, drilling, cutting and polishing. There is also a demand for them in high-power lasers and electronic applications in transistors. These products don't have the same healing energy as diamonds that are produced by a geological process.

Because crystals originate within the body of the planet, they can be described as the earths DNA, which holds within it the development of our planet over millions of years and of course, they contain the energy of powerful forces that shaped them. Crystals have the ability to absorb, conserve, focus and emit energy, especially on an electromagnetic waveband. This is exciting because the cells within our bodies emit weak electromagnetic fields called biophotons, and these help the cells communicate with each other, so when the crystals are placed on or near the human body, electromagnetic radiation from the crystal affects these biophotons and this process can change brain patterns. On a cellular level, crystals can stimulate tissues and organs, while also affecting the flow of energy in the meridians and Chakras.

Crystals are normally used in conjunction with other forms of Energy Healing, such as Reiki. When it comes to choosing a crystal, it is best to buy it from a shop or at a mind, body and spirit fair. You should always use your own intuition, because by handling the crystal, your own subtle body can feel its vibration. The crystal's attraction is a form of intuitive intelligence that connects to your mind.

Crystals come in two forms: raw and polished. The stones get the shiny polished look by being tumbled in a barrel with a product called "grind". There are various stages to the polishing, starting with a coarse grind, then a finer one and eventually a rock polish that is used to create the smooth stone. It does not matter if you use raw crystals or polished ones, as they all have the same energy.

Over time you will build up a selection of crystals, each one will be used for a different purpose. The following is just a short guide that shows which crystal is used for which ailment.

10: Crystal Healing

Quartz

This crystal comes in many colours and shapes. Clear quartz can be used for most conditions; it stimulates the immune system and balances the Chakras. It can be held during meditation to connect to higher levels of spiritual consciousness. In healing, it attunes itself to the energy required to combat the sickness.

Rose quartz is the stone of love. It can mend a broken heart and it draws off any negative energy that may have built up in the Heart Chakra from grief or break up of a relationship and it replaces it with love. It is also said to increase fertility.

Smoky Quartz

This is a brownish or blackish colour, although sometimes it can be as light as yellow. It can be used for problems in the central area of the body, especially the abdomen and hips. It relieves pain and is of benefit to the reproductive system.

Lapis Lazuli

This is a dark blue crystal with white and gold flecks. It is a spiritual stone that is associated with the upper Chakras of the Throat, Third Eye and Crown. The healing benefits include the alleviation of migraines, headaches and sore throats. It is also good for people who suffer with insomnia and vertigo; Lapis Lazuli can draw out tension and anxiety. It will activate communication and assist people who are introverted and shy. Because of its communication qualities, it is ideal for focusing on while meditating.

Amethyst
This is one of the more common crystals, and it is a wonderful healing stone, known for its calming and stabilising effect on the mind. It is used to dispel anger and anxiety, and for promoting love and compassion.

Shungite
Shungite is pronounced "shunkite" and until recently, it was unknown outside Russia, where it is mined in the Republic of Karelia, a region in the northwest, close to the border with Finland. This is the only place on earth where it can be found. The deposit of shungite extends over an area of 3,475 square miles.

Although similar in appearance to coal, there are significant differences between coal and shungite. Coal was formed between 300 and 600 million years ago, and that is about 1.5 billion years later than shungite. It is the molecular makeup of shungite that makes it such a special healing stone. The energy within shungite is said to absorb and eliminate anything that is damaging to human life, and it has active metaphysical properties with strong healing powers. It is a powerful shield for protection against electromagnetic radiation from electrical equipment, computers, microwaves, televisions and mobile phones.

There are three types of shungite, the first and most scarce is silver shungite, which accounts for only one per cent of all shungite. Silver shungite contains ninety-eight per cent carbon. The second type is black shungite, which contains sixty-four per cent carbon, and finally the third type is grey shungite, which has thirty per cent carbon content.

10: Crystal Healing

Shungite is a very versatile crystal stone as it can be used in a similar way to that of other crystals, but it is also useful for grounding during meditation. You can put a piece of shungite into a glass of water and leave it for a while, so that the healing properties of the stone are absorbed by the water. This can be used for general well-being, but it has also been used as a holistic healing treatment for depression and for cancer. Packets of shungite stones for water filters are readily available for purchase on the internet.

There is a room in a Russian hospital that has its walls painted with shungite, and recently a similar room has been built in Paris. Its floor and walls are covered in shungite tiles and the ceiling contains a layer of powdered shungite. This room is used as a complementary therapeutic place for stimulating self-healing. For more detailed information on shungite, I recommend reading "Shungite" by Regina Martino.

Using Crystals for Healing Purposes

When it comes to healing with crystals, there are various options. For instance, a crystal can be placed directly on the area of pain or illness, and then the healer tunes into the crystal and places his hand over the crystal, allowing the healing energy to flow through the crystal into the place where the healing is needed. Alternatively, by placing the crystals on each of the Chakras, you can bring harmony and balance to the patient. Intuition is useful when deciding where to place the crystals during healing.

In the home or workplace, crystals can be used for protection and harmony, and you should use your intuition to work out where to put your crystals. A more practical use of crystals is to place a crystal close to computers, to neutralize electromagnetic smog, which is a subtle but detectable electromagnetic field that can have an adverse effect on some people. This comes from cell phones microwaves, televisions and power cables as well as computers. A good crystal for this protection against electromagnetic smog is Amazonite, which comes in both blue and green colours. If a computer starts playing up for some reason, place small pieces of blue lace agate on or near it to calm it down. Incidentally, I have also found children should not be allowed near computers, they seem to have an effect on the computer that usually results in the computer throwing a wobbly.

A Crystal Grid

A crystal grid is a means of sending a continuous healing energy to those who have long term physical or mental issues. The best crystals for making a crystal grid are clear quartz. There are various ways to create a crystal grid, but they all have a central crystal with a number of crystals surrounding it. Clear quartz crystals normally have one end that comes to a point – similar to a wand – and the energy is transmitted from the point. The size of the grid can be from six to twelve inches in diameter. The outer crystals will have the points facing the centre, so the energy is focused on the central crystal. You can use up to twelve surrounding crystals, as long as they are all spaced evenly. Then you put a list of names or photographs of those who need to receive the healing on the table below the central crystal.

To charge the grid, you need to use a crystal wand, which is a long crystal with a point on one end. You need to

10: Crystal Healing

take care and use such wands with great respect, as they can emit a great deal of energy. They always remind me of the light sabres that you see in Star Wars films. So you need to keep such wands safe and keep them away from children. Start by holding the wand in your dominant hand, which is the one you write with, and imagine the energy flowing down your arm to the tip of the wand. Point the wand at the central crystal and move the energy beam up to an outer crystal, then across to the next outer crystal and back down to the central crystal, repeat the process until all crystals have been charged. A mantra can be said while charging the crystals. Once the crystal grid is charged, it will send out continuous healing.

The best place to keep your crystal grid is on a flat surface where it won't be disturbed.

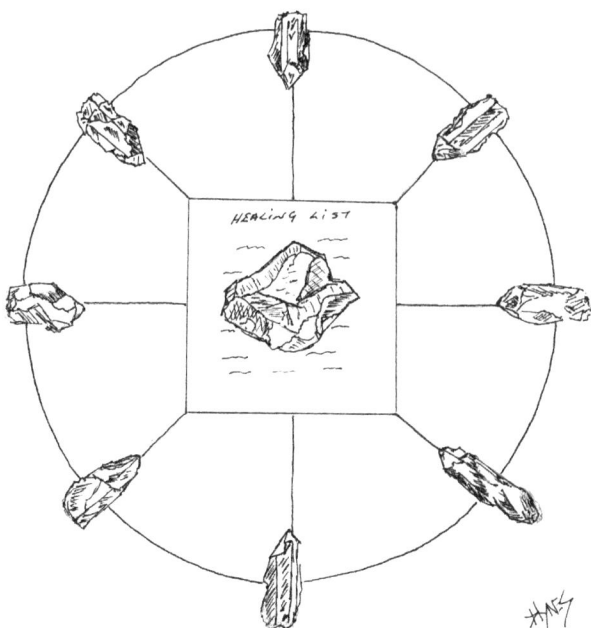

Energy Healing in Focus

Useful Crystal Information

Preparing Crystals

When you first acquire your crystals, it is important that you cleanse them to remove any negative energy from the people who may have handled them before, because when you cleanse them, you return them to their original energetic frequency. The most common way to cleanse crystals is to wash them under running water. However, there are some crystals that can be damaged by the water; for instance, salt crystals, malachite and selenite shouldn't come into contact with water. There are others that shouldn't be washed so you need to ask about this when you buy your crystal. However, most can be washed. My friend Sasha suggests collecting a bit of rain water for this purpose rather than using what comes out of the tap. Another alternative is to buy a bottle of decent mineral water and use that.

After washing your crystals, leave them to dry in natural daylight, but avoid direct sunlight. I have some friends who are white witches, and they like to place their crystals under the light of the full moon, while others like to leave their crystals for twenty-four hours so they get the benefit of both sunlight and moonlight.

Once your crystals have been cleansed they can be charged, and this can be done by simply placing your hand over the crystal and given it a blast of healing energy. Use your intuition to know when your crystals need cleansing and recharging. I always wash my healing crystals before and after a healing session in order to remove any negative energy. The crystals on your healing grid do not require cleansing because by charging them you are cleansing them.

10: Crystal Healing

Meditating with Crystals

Meditating with crystals helps you to attune to the crystal's energy and in time you will discover which your favourite meditation crystal is. As with all meditations, you need to find a place where you won't be disturbed. Settle down, holding the crystal loosely in your hand, or you can hold a crystal in each hand.

- Settle into a quiet state, close your eyes and relax your body, take three deep breaths, then settle into a steady rhythm with your breathing.
- Feel the energy of the crystal moving up your arms and into the Heart Chakra, then spreading out through your body.
- After a while you will not even be aware that you have the crystals in your hands, you will have blended in completely.

Eleven: Shamanic Healing

The word shaman can be used to describe ancient spiritual practices among indigenous cultures worldwide, and in recent times there has been a revival in interest in shamanism and the shamanic practice. The traditional shaman is a spiritual and ceremonial leader of the tribe, and he is not so much responsible for any one individual but for the community he represents. He is seen as an intermediary between the human and the spirit world, and I suppose you could say he is somewhere between a witch doctor, healer, wise man, councillor and adviser for the tribe or community. But today you don't have to live in a remote location to be a shaman, and your tribe or community are those around you who look up to you and respect your views.

In the days before radio, television and instant communication with people in distant lands via Skype and mobile phones, people lived within their own communities. Even today, you can visit Cornwall and find people who have never ventured outside the county, and I expect there are similar people in Scotland and Wales. In a close community, everyone fits together like the pieces in a giant jigsaw puzzle, and the role of the shaman is to protect the community by acting as an intermediary between the spirits of the earth, animals, weather and crops.

Humans were once totally dependent on the forces of nature, so it was the shaman's duty to predict problems before they came to pass, and to find ways of preventing them from occurring. An example of a natural disaster of this kind can occur when indigenous people rely upon one main source of food, and the obvious example of this occurred in Ireland in the middle of the nineteenth century, when the populace relied upon potatoes as the staple crop. When potato blight ravaged the crop, over a million people died from starvation and millions more left Ireland to make lives for themselves in other lands. Did shamans see this disaster coming? They probably did, but without the ability to broadcast on a large scale in those days, and with the likelihood of being dismissed as lunatics, they didn't get their message out to the bulk of the people.

The shaman's feet span two worlds, because he or she is aware of the spiritual side of life at all times. One aspect of shamanic belief is that every living creature has a spirit, and because we are also spiritual beings, it is possible for us to connect to animals as well as to earth energies. Animal spirits can travel between the visible and the invisible worlds. Shamanism is not a religion, so there is no hierarchy of priests and bishops. Shamans respect all life and they believe we can live in harmony with the earth and sky. They believe that all life is sacred, and that it should be treated with reverence and respect.

What Shamans Do

The shaman can send his spirit on a journey to communicate with other spirits in order to determine why a crop is failing or if there will be a drought. As well as communicating with the earth and animal spirits, the shaman can commune with his ancestors and gods. Shamanic journeying is a method of travelling to other realms, and it is this gift that makes the shaman unique in the community.

Ritual and costumes are important for the journeying, so eagle feathers, skins, bones and designs are seen as a way of linking with spirit. The shaman induces a trance state, which is assisted by the drum beats, rattles, dancing, herbs and incense. The shaman will contact a guide who is a power animal, and this may be an eagle, wolf, bear, horse, owl or any other animal. Fasting is another traditional means of increasing spiritual awareness, as it can alter consciousness and allow the shaman to enter the trance state more easily.

The Healer

The first type of shaman is the healer, who journeys to the upper or lower worlds to seek help for the sick. He may also use remedies made from herbs and other plants, which can be taken orally as tea or can be made into poultices and ointments.

The Soul Retriever

The second type of shaman is the soul retriever. Certain illnesses have a specifically spiritual component that may respond to shamanic healing techniques where other methods have failed. Such things might be psychological problems like addictions, depression and anxiety. Those who lose the will to live usually become despondent as a result of some ongoing traumatic experience. Children who are bullied at school, or people returning from war who are left untreated, can become so low that they end up taking their own lives.

Some of the symptoms of soul-loss are feelings of being fragmented, of not being whole, or feeling like a satellite that is forever destined to orbit a planet, looking down at it and seeing its beauty but never allowed to become part of it. This could be described as a kind of "Lady of Shallot" syndrome. Some feel unable to love or to feel loved, while others lack drive, feel negative, have suicidal tendencies, feel chronically depressed, lonely and melancholy. As long as this empty space remains in the soul, the patient cannot return to the state of fullness to which we are all entitled.

The shaman, with the assistance of his spiritual helpers, enters into a relationship with the missing, fragmented parts of the person's soul, which may have taken refuge in the lower worlds, where they may be among the animal spirits who are caring for it. A "soul-part" may also be located in the middle world of dream and in the company of an ancestor. Once the soul is restored, the shaman instructs the patient on how to reintegrate these lost soul-parts, thus assuring successful and permanent reunion.

The Spiritual Healer

The third type of shaman is the spiritual healer and he is similar to what we call psychologists or psychiatrists. These are people who deal with anger, frustration, jealousy, hate and prejudice. When the shaman treats a patient, he may use herbs as well as music in the healing. This enables the shaman to lead the patient into a semi-hypnotic state, while the shaman goes into trance in order to remove the causes of the issues.

The Messenger Shaman

The fourth type of shaman is the messenger who brings back information for individuals in a similar way to that of a spiritual medium.

Twelve: Aromatherapy and Magnets

Energy Healing in Focus

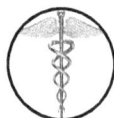

Although not strictly a form of Energy Healing, aromatherapy can play an important part when it comes to healing. The use of oils extracted from plants has been around for a long time. For example, in the Book of Genesis, Adam and Eve were in a garden filled with the scents of flowers, trees and plants. In the Book of Exodus, God gave Moses a recipe for making holy anointing oil, and the ingredients included myrrh, cassia, cinnamon and olive oil. Frankincense is oil that is frequently mentioned in the bible, and of course, it was given to Christ at the time of his birth. Research has shown that frankincense stimulates the part of the brain that controls emotions.

> *The bible contains over 600 references to essential oils and aromatic plants*

- Sandalwood has a calming and emotionally balancing effect, and it can be used to help unwind in stressful situations.
- Cinnamon promotes a healthy immune system.
- Galbanum is good for opening up for spiritual communication, and when used alongside frankincense in meditation, it increases awareness.
- Myrrh is a powerful antioxidant that can promote a healthy skin.
- Cedar wood has an earthy aroma that gives a sense of security.

Oils were also used in ancient Egypt, and the "Seven Sacred Oils", one of which is cedar wood, were used daily in temple ritual, funerary rites, cosmetics and medicines. The temple statues were anointed daily with perfume.

In the Christian churches, the burning of incense was rooted in the earlier traditions of Judaism. Some say it is a symbol of the prayers of the faithful rising to heaven. In the middle ages the burning of incense in church had the additional benefit of masking the smell of the unwashed congregation! However, the religious significance of anointing people with holy oil was to symbolise the Holy Spirit coming upon them to divinely empower them. The Disciples of Christ anointed the sick with holy oil and healed them in the name of Jesus, so once more, oil symbolised the soothing and healing presence of the Holy Spirit. The Holy Catholic sacrament of anointing the sick (Extreme Unction) is performed on seriously ill people to give them spiritual and physical strength in preparation for heaven. When this is used in confession and when receiving the Eucharist, it is called "Last Rites".

> *When my own dear mother was close to death, the village priest was called to administer the Last Rites. She recovered and eventually outlived the priest!*

There are hundreds of essential oils that the professional aromatherapist can use for specific ailments. A wide range of conditions may benefit from aromatherapy, and some oils are used as a preventive as well as a cure. As this is a holistic way of treating a patient, the practitioner will take into account the patient's lifestyle as well as the symptoms, before the aromatherapist decides which oils are most suitable. Several essential oils may be blended into a base-oil, which is then put directly onto the patient's skin.

> *Essential oils are extremely concentrated, so they are used in very small quantities and always blended into a base-oil. This base oil is selected for its absorption and nutrient qualities.*

Massage
One method for the application of oils can be massage, which is relaxing in itself, while allowing the oil to sink into the skin.

Bathing
One can take a bath with a few drops of essential oil in the water, as the vapours will be inhaled while the body has a good soak.

12: Aromatherapy & Magnets

Inhalation

Inhalation is the most direct means of getting the vapour to the brain. In this case, put a few drops of oil in a bowl of hot water and ask the patient to sit with his face over the bowl, with a towel covering his head so the vapours do not escape. Another way of inhalation is to place a few drops on a pillow before you going to bed. Only administer inhalation treatments with approval from the patient's doctor, and in your thorough knowledge of the essential oil being used. For one thing, the person may have respiratory issues or intolerances that may flare up when triggered by certain vapours.

Beauty Treatments

Oils that are used in hair treatments are sometimes known as serums, and in this case, the diluted oil can be massaged into the scalp before wrapping the hair in a warm towel and allowing the oil to penetrate for an hour or two. Massaging cream into the face is a form of aromatherapy that you can give yourself every day. Massaging in foot cream is another such method.

Finally, it is worth mentioning again that in general, some oils may have an adverse effect, and they should only be used under the guidance of a professional aromatherapist.

HEALING WITH MAGNETS

The human body is mostly made up of water molecules that consist of hydrogen and oxygen atoms, and at the centre of each hydrogen atom is a proton. Protons are like tiny magnets and they are sensitive to other magnetic fields. It is these protons that allow Magnetic Resonance Imaging (MRI) to produce detailed images of the inside of the body. Within our physical body, we generate our own magnetic field, and by stimulating these electro-magnetic fields, it is possible to assist the mending of broken bones.

The use of magnetism is growing, and it is quite common for people to wear magnetic bracelets for pain relief, especially arthritis, and these bracelets can be very stylish and decorative. This isn't a case of imagination, because there have been good reports of people helping arthritic pets by attaching magnetic bracelets to their collars.

GEOPATHIC STRESS

Geopathic stress is a hidden enemy that we cannot see. When the earth's energy changes, it causes geopathic stress; the brain interacts with this stress and it can weaken the immune system. Therefore, if you happen to live above an underground stream (which can generate a weak electric field) and have an electric pylon or power cables above your house, these two can have a detrimental affect on your health due to the negative energy they produce. Electro-magnetic and geopathic stress can be detected by dowsing.

More than 4,000 years ago, the Chinese recognised destructive earth vibrations and called them "dragon lines". They warned against building houses on such stressful sites. The Chinese say that living with a stream behind or below one's house causes extremely bad Feng Shui, which affects the health and finances of all who live there.

Thirteen:
Spiritual Healing

Energy Healing in Focus

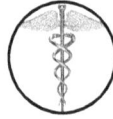

There are some medical conditions that cannot be cured by traditional medical practices and too often we hear the words, "There is nothing more we can do". At that stage we can accept the inevitable and wait for the Grim Reaper, or we can seek a holistic cure. There are countless accounts of people who have been written off, who then make miraculous recoveries, and spiritual healers can claim a fair share of success where these cases are concerned.

We all have a soul and spirit that cannot be destroyed by any physical thing because it is immortal. Once we accept this fact, we can live without fear of sickness or death. We instinctively know that there is something more to existence than what we can see and feel.

> *I am Love. You are Love. All is Love.*
>
> *We are part of the Divine, and*
>
> *there is a spark of divinity in all of us*

As we pass through life in a physical or spiritual form, we are on the road to the state of ultimate perfection. That does not mean we will reach the highest mountain, because there are others who are greater than us. The ascended masters and angels are above us, and the Divine Spirit / God is above them. Our spiritual selves don't feel put out at our occupation of a lesser place than the angels and the Divine. When we learn to accept

13: Spiritual Healing

our place in the "great plan" we become one, as part of the Divine / God.

Spiritualism teaches that we can transcend death and that we will still have a part to play in helping others achieve their spiritual goals thereafter. During our existence in the physical state, we can call upon those who have passed over to help us to heal ourselves and our fellow man. We are not alone even when we are in the darkest dungeon or the loneliest place, as we are always supported by our Guardian Angel and Spiritual Helpers. These angels and guides will help us if we ask them to, but we always have free will, and we don't have to accept their help if we decide that we don't want it. They will respect our decisions and won't interfere.

When we die, our Soul and Spirit leaves the physical body. The Soul is the essence of who we are as a person, and it is what makes us individual. The Spirit is the part of us that relates to God. We are not spirit - but we do have a spirit. The evil that others do to us can kill the body but not the soul, so there is always hope.

Prayer
Spiritual healing comes in different ways and the simplest way is through the power of prayer. This method of healing is a direct request to the Divine / God for help to intercede in a specific situation. It is a form of communication; so all we have to do is ask. We do not need to use a set formula of words that have no meaning to us, because it is the passion behind the prayer that matters. God will answer prayers that are in agreement with his will, and while the answer will not always be "yes", it *will* be in our best interest.

Sometimes we don't want to bother God, so we may pray to saints and ascended masters. By praying to a saint we feel a more personal connection. Many people will have their own favourite saint.

Does praying through an intermediary make a difference? I don't think so. Irrespective of what kind of spiritual healing we use, the source of the healing energy ultimately comes from God / the Divine.

Spiritualism

Spiritualism is a religion that employs ministers and that carries out services in places of worship. Most cities and large towns will have one or more spiritualist churches. Spiritualists are in direct communication with the spirit of those who have crossed over to the other side.

Most spiritual healers start out as spiritual mediums, and progress naturally into using their connection to spirit to heal. The majority of spiritual healers get on quietly with their job without seeking the fame or celebrity status that some psychic mediums attract. With patience and training, anyone can develop their psychic skills and become a spiritual healer, but there are a number who have a natural psychic gift, and such gifts tend to run in families and pass through the generations. Some psychics hear people talking to them from the other side, which is known as clairaudience, while others see things (clairvoyance) or sense them in the form of clairsentience.

Before spiritual healers can heal, they need to make contact with, or blend with, their spirit helpers or guides. To heal spiritually, we need the divine light that is within us to be brought to the surface. As I said at the beginning of this book, everything is energy, and energy vibrates at different frequencies, so a stone contains a lower frequency than a plant, and the plant is lower than an animal. The spirit world vibrates at a higher level than mankind, which means that when we want to connect with spirit we need to raise our vibration, and for spirit to lowers theirs. This allows us to adjust our level of awareness and be in tune with spirit.

The Levels of Consciousness

The first level of consciousness is the Beta state, which is our normal waking state. It's the state where we think and reason, function on a daily basis, drive a car, operate machinery, play sport and so on. Beta brain-waves operate at 14 cps (cycles per second) and above.

The next level is the Alpha state, which is regarded as the subconscious state. We are in this state of awareness when asleep – although we may also drift into this state when we are awake but day-dreaming. Meditation takes place in the Alpha state of consciousness, whereby we are not asleep but very relaxed. The Alpha brain waves operate between 7cps to 14cps. The mind is much calmer at this stage, so it is where spiritual mediums connect to spirit.

For connecting on a deeper psychic and spiritual level, the Theta state of awareness is required, the brain waves at this level being between 4cps to 7cps. There isn't any point in a psychic or spiritual medium going to this level, because they need to be alert in order to communicate their message or give healing to their client. The Theta state is where our dreams become the means of communication.

Energy Healing in Focus

The final condition is the Delta state, which operates at 0cps to 4cps, and this is total unconsciousness.

As the spiritual healers start to relax, their minds move into the Alpha state of awareness, which also means that the logical Beta state is lessened. Once in the Alpha state, the medium or healer raises his conscious state (vibrations) and the spirit lowers theirs until they blend. It takes practice and patience to reach this stage of communication with spirit, and there has to be co-operation on both sides. One of the obstacles to achieving this blending is the difficulty we may have in being able to clear our minds and relax, but if we make the effort, we can do it because the spirit world wants to help us.

The spiritual healer will normally have more than one guide. I have a strong male guide and a gentle female guide for healing. The male guide is easier to feel due to his strong presence, while the female is more subtle. They know which of them will step forward to assist in the healing, and I only have to trust that they know what they are doing.

Aggressive conditions like cancer need a different approach to mental problems, so the strong guide would help with the cancer, while the gentle one would help with mental problems. The conditions for spiritual healing are similar to those of Energy Healing, and the only exception that I can find is that spirits like fresh flowers. You need a quiet place where you won't be interrupted, and which is warm but not too hot. Before the patient arrives, you need to give notice to spirit of your intention to heal, as they like to know this in advance. You can give this notice several hours or even days beforehand. As with all healing, we cannot guarantee to heal, but we know that the process will not do anything to harm the patient.

13: Spiritual Healing

The normal position for the patient is sitting in an upright chair, and the spiritual healer will ask the patient if it is all right to touch them with his or her hands. The healer may touch the patient on the back or shoulder, or directly where the problem is located. The spiritual healer imagines a hollow tube within himself, with the healing energy coming down from the Universe, through the healer's body, through his hands and into the patient. The person receiving the healing may be aware of intense heat coming from the healer and of the power surrounding him.

The healer may want to talk to the patient during the healing, and he may pass on anything he intuitively picks up. The spiritual energy is very similar to Reiki energy, as all these energies derive from the same source.

Trance Healing

Another type of spiritual healing is trance healing. There is some confusion about the word trance because in trance healing the healer is not possessed by the spirit. He is aware of what is happening and he is in control of the situation all the time, although trance takes place in the lower end of the Alpha and the Theta states of awareness. If the trance healer was in the Delta state, he would be unconscious and have no control over spirit, which means that spirit would not be able carry out the healing. It is the trance healer who allows spirit to function. So trance healing itself is similar to spiritual healing, since the trance healer can still communicate with the patient during the healing.

The spiritual medium and the trance healer both connect with spirit by attuning and blending, but once they have blended, there is a difference between the medium and the trance healer. The medium increases his awareness of spirit (active communication) because he or she needs to receive and relay messages, while the trance healer needs to be still (passive communication) and allow the spirit to take over the healing without interfering.

This really is gradual, so at first the spiritual element may only be twenty per cent, then as the healer becomes relaxed and comfortable, it will increase to eighty per cent, but never to a hundred per cent. Some of the early indications of being in trance are change in the healer's breathing, which may become deeper or shallower. There will be a change in body temperature, and the patient may notice that the healer looks as though his face is shaded by cobwebs (overshadowing) and there may be a change in the emotional state. The medium's own mind will become more passive so that he can enable spirit to function. The secret is to suppress the logical mind and surrender to the spirit that is coming in to give healing.

13: Spiritual Healing

Once in a complete trance state, observers may notice psychic changes in the trance healer. I have seen an old lady's face change into that of a man, her chin became recessed, her nose more pointed and her voice deeper. Her mannerisms were also different, so she was a totally different person while carrying out trance healing. I have also seen trance mediums giving lectures in trance, one gentleman with a broad Scottish accent changing to a German accent, and his features changing from soft to rugged. Another medium had a very bad cough and we weren't sure that he could give the lecture at all, but when he was in trance there was no sign of his cough, and he managed to talk for forty minutes without having to cough once, while his voice and personality also changed.

Psychic Surgery

Finally, we have the psychic surgeon. Psychic surgery has a bad reputation due to the large number of fake psychic surgeons in the Philippines and South America. These confidence tricksters create the illusion of performing surgery with their bare hands by using fake blood and animal parts. Despite this, there are reputable people who carry out psychic surgery and I have seen these people at work. A genuine psychic surgeon will always advise you to consult your doctor and to continue to take whatever medicines your doctor has prescribed. As with all spiritual healing, psychic surgeons are complementary therapists, in that they work alongside the traditional medical profession.

The psychic surgeon goes into the trance state, and once in trance, he or she will have a team of spirit doctors or surgeons to assist with the healing. This team of doctors and surgeons are spirits who were once actual doctors and surgeons when they were in this life. As with surgery in this life, doctors who specialise in different ailments are used in the spirit world.

The psychic surgeon will place his hands above the area that needs healing, though the surgery is completely non-intrusive and there is no requirement for the patient to remove any clothing. Some people who have had psychic surgery report that that felt as though work has been done to their organs even though the healer's hands didn't touch their body.

Aura Clearing – With Reiki

Something similar to psychic surgery is aura clearing. As a Reiki master and teacher I have performed this on rare occasions when everything else has failed, and because it is so powerful, it should be shown respect. Aura clearing can help with deep-rooted emotional problems, addictions and physical health problems. The clearing / surgery works within the energy field around the patient.

The first step is to give the cause of the problem an identity, as this helps both healer and patient to have a point to focus on, and after this, the problem can be released.

* I ask the patient to think about the issue that he or she wants healed, but he doesn't have to say what is on his mind, as he just needs to think about it.
* Then I ask, "Do you want to be healed?" This is important because it sets out the intention of both the healer and the patient.
* Next, I ask the patient to close his eyes and to focus, asking what part of the body the problem is in, so

that we can give it an identity. This spot is normally where the patient feels pain or a sense of loss.

- I will then ask what shape it is, for example, is it round, oval, square or cubic.
- Then I ask the patient to describe the texture, and say whether it is soft, bobbled, rough or sharp.
- Finally, I ask how much the ailment weighs.

The individual may not be able to describe all these things, but he will describe some of them and it is a visual way to give the problem form.

* * *

The Reiki healer then goes through a routine that includes the use of sacred symbols and words that focus his or her energy. Then he symbolically extends the fingers on his healing hand to about twelve inches above the body, and with the fingers extended, he reaches into the patient's aura and - symbolically - removes the object or problem. It may take a few attempts before it is gone, and we have to rely on intuition to know when this has happened.

This aura clearing is normally done alongside a complete Reiki healing session. After it is complete, we ask the patient if the problem has gone, and while it may sometimes still be there, it should be smaller and lighter. In that case another session at a later date may be required.

Remember that no matter how many times you heal some-thing, unless you get rid of the *cause* of the ailment, it will return.

Fourteen: Colour

Colour is something that we take for granted, without realising the powerful effect that it has on our subconscious. Each colour has a different energy vibration, and of course, each chakra has its own colour.

Chakra	Colour
Crown	Violet
Third Eye (also known as Brow)	Purple or dark blue
Throat	Light Blue or turquoise
Heart	Green
Solar Plexus	Yellow
Sacral	Orange
Base (also known as Root)	Red

The Colour Red can be used when a display of power or strength is needed. For instance, when Prime Minister Theresa May went to visit President Donald Trump in America, for their first meeting she wore a bright red suit, and he wore a red tie of a similar shade. A high percentage of world flags have red somewhere in them, and China uses red for its flag as an indication of its power. So did the old Soviet Union, and so does Russia today. Red is also a colour of protection, so people are often reluctant to open a red door.

On a personal note, I have a garage at the back of my house that is accessible from a service lane at the rear of the property. I have always painted the garage door red, so while some of my neighbours have had graffiti painted on their doors at some point in time, I have been spared by the wannabe Banksy clones. Red is an empowering colour, so if you want to feel powerful in a subtle way, why not wear red underwear?

Orange is the colour of creativity and spontaneity; it is less harsh than red and has a warm feel about it. It is a favourite colour of artists, particularly impressionist painters.

Yellow is a cheerful, happy colour that shows that we are approachable and willing to help, which reminds me of the "yellow coats" who work at the Butlins holiday camps. Some Buddhist monks wear yellow, as did many of the "flower children" of the 1970s. It is a colour of peace and acceptance. It is also associated with teaching, so if you have information to impart to others, wear something yellow.

Light Green is the colour of the Heart Chakra, and this is where we connect to our fellow beings through love and compassion. If you want to wear your heart on your sleeve, then light green is the colour for you. There are some beautiful, light green, precious stones that can be worn as jewellery, and these will enhance the gentle side of the wearer's personality.

Light Blue is the colour for you if you have difficulty in expressing yourself verbally. A man who is dressing before going for a job interview should put on a light blue shirt or tie, as this helps him to project his personality. Similarly, the female interviewee might choose a light blue blouse. You could sit and look at a postcard of a light blue sea as an exercise in visualisation in the hours before the interview. Light blue is also the colour that helps to connect to the spiritual plane.

Purple is the colour of inner wisdom, and it is associated with the priesthood in several religions. It is the gateway to sacred knowledge. Before the days of aniline dyes, purple could only be created by soaking cloth in water containing the ground-up shells of a particularly rare sea creature. It was so precious that purple cloth was never thrown away, and it was made into new garments for each new king, emperor or person of power. Thus, purple was known as the colour of wealth, royalty and status. During the season of Lent, some Catholic churches cover religious images with purple cloths, and these are unveiled on Good Friday for the veneration of the cross. This colour is also used to signify penance and mourning in the church.

Using Colour while Meditating
Before you start, pick the colour that will help you achieve balance in your life. If you focus and visualise the colour while meditating, you can draw the energy associated with the colour into your body. If you need to feel up-lifted and optimistic, yellow is a good colour to choose, but if you feel stressed, you should choose light green to bring peace and harmony into your life.

As an example, if I had confidence issues, I would pick the colour yellow or envisage a yellow ball or even a banana. I would close my eyes and imagine the yellow ball between the palms of my hands, and see it as being as bright as the sun. I would feel the energy of the ball of yellow and then I would move the ball of light into my Solar Plexus Chakra.

Fifteen: Sound

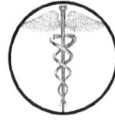

Words

In the Gospel of St John, it says, "In the beginning was the Word and the Word was with God and the Word was God and the Word was made flesh." So we now know that a word is a sound, and each sound has its own unique vibration.

Sound Therapy

Sound has been used from the beginning of history to create certain moods. In medieval times, the chanting of the monks was used to uplift the spirit, while the drumming of the shaman creates a trance-like state. There are cases where the sound waves of recitation of the holy Quran (Holy Book of the Muslim Religion) have cured diseases that were incurable by normal medical means. The use of sound frequency for healing purposes has grown in popularity in recent years and it can be used for sleeping disorders and even difficult problems such as attention deficit disorders, where it helps to slow down the brain's activity. It is said that sound therapy can help children with dyslexia, because the sounds used can help to synchronise the two hemispheres of the brain. A variety of instruments can be used, including Australian didgeridoos!

The British Academy of Sound Therapy (BAST) uses sound therapy to balance the body's energy fields. The starting point is for the therapist to ask the client about his medical history and any current problems, before using drums, bells, singing bowls, gongs, tuning forks and the human voice. Apparently, this is particularly useful for clients who feel themselves to be under stress, but it is also said to be helpful with anxiety, tinnitus, fertility issues, irritable bowel and chronic fatigue syndromes. Usually, the improvement in mood and health lasts for some time after the treatment but the patient will need occasional top-ups.

Tibetan Singing Bowls

There is little ancient writing about singing bowls, but according to oral tradition, they date back to the time of Buddha Shakyamui (560 - 480 BC)

Singing bowls are usually made of brass or bronze, and they are "played" by running a padded mallet around the inner or outer rim of the bowl, or by striking the bowl to make it ring. I have headed this section "Tibetan Singing Bowls", but they have long been known all over the Orient. They are used in chanting to signal the start or the end of the session or to change some part of the activity during it, such as changing from a sitting meditation to a walking one. They are used in meditation and yoga, for religious purposes, Reiki, chakra balancing and music.

Healing Tuning Forks

Healing tuning forks resonate at a specific, constant pitch when set to vibrate by striking against a surface. The pitch of each tuning fork depends on the length and mass of the two prongs. On the base of each fork there is a node, which is a point of no vibration, and this allows the user the hold the fork without dampening the vibration. The sounds are used in much the same way as the singing bowls, as they can be used for meditation, relaxation and perhaps as an aid to other forms of healing.

Sound as a Diagnostic Tool

High frequency sound pulses that are similar to sonar are used in medicine for diagnostic purposes, the most common being the ultrasound scanner that can produce an image of the foetus as it develops in the womb. Ultrasound can also be used for more than mere imaging, because neurosurgeons now use a device called a cavitron ultrasonic surgical aspirator (CUSA) to remove brain tumours that once were thought to be inoperable. They do this by sending sound waves through the slender tip of the CUSA probe, and the vibration shatters any section of the tumour that it touches, while the remaining fragments are flushed out of the brain with a saline solution. These are just some of the uses of sound in conventional medicine.

15: Sound

Music

Listening to music is still one of the most relaxing ways to chill out, and my favourite music for meditating is *"Syllabus of Magic"* by Neil H. This music seems to take me to another dimension.

When my son was a teenager he was heavily into his music, and as a would-be DJ, he had a twin turntable for mixing tunes, so he and his mates would spend time in his room playing on his turntables. While my wife and I were sitting downstairs and watching the television, we couldn't hear the music, but we could feel the boom, boom vibration throughout the house. On one occasion after repeated requests for him to turn the sound down, I went to the fuse panel and removed the fuse to the upstairs power circuit. This caused him some confusion, because he thought there had been a power cut, but when he came downstairs everything was normal and we were watching television. Not long after that, his mates went home and we enjoyed a peaceful night!

The idea behind the therapeutic use of sound is either to calm and relax the mind and the brain or to stimulate it, depending upon what is required. As we can see, sounds and music are a matter of personal preference, but one sound that everyone seems to like is the sound of waves gently breaking on a pebble beach.

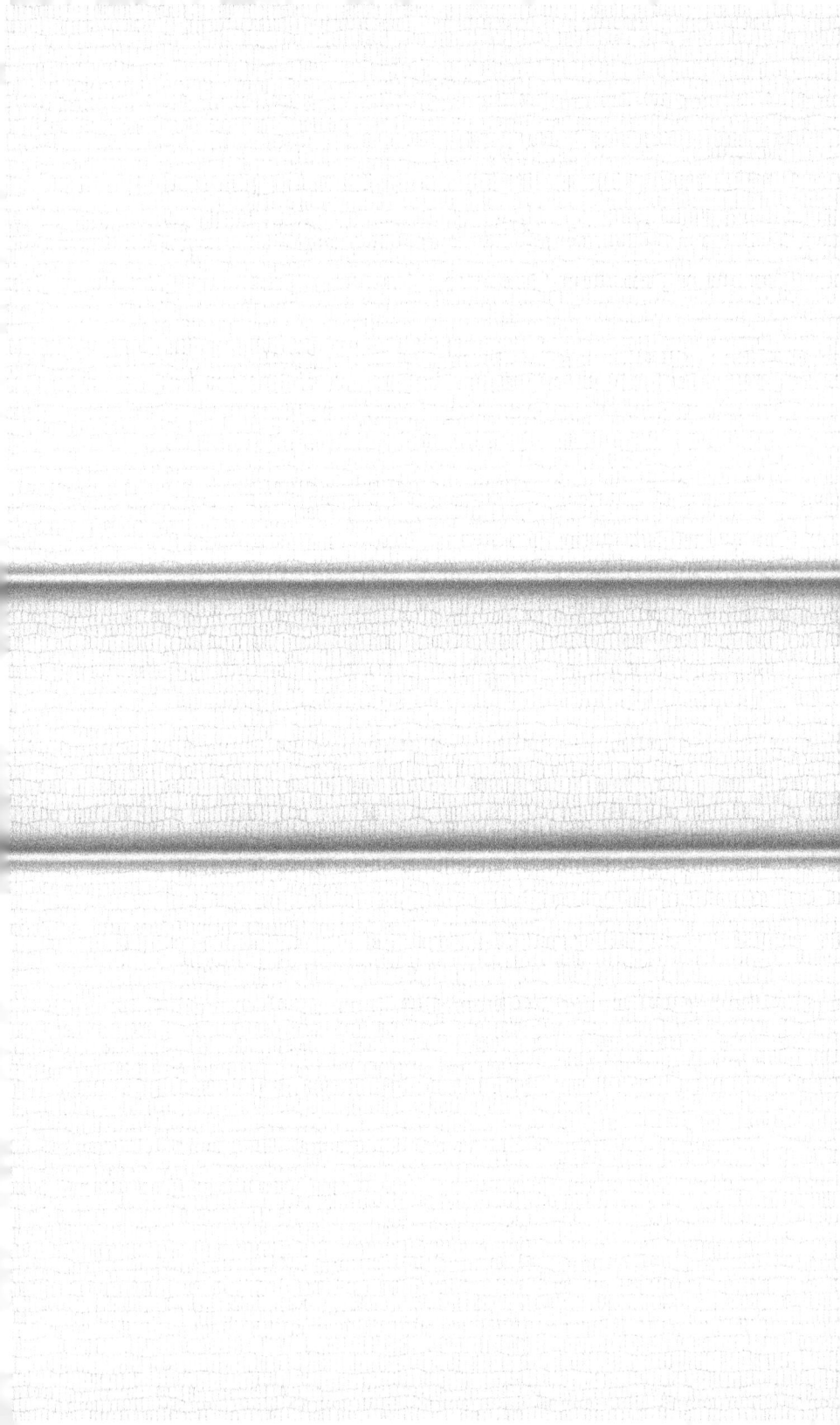

Sixteen:
A Healthy Lifestyle

Energy Healing in Focus

We cannot separate our physical health from our mental health, and the holistic approach to healing is to treat the Mind, Body and Spirit together. We can start by decluttering our lives, and letting go of things that no longer serve a purpose; this is not a call for everyone to go out and get divorced or change their job, although there may be some who need to make these changes. Everything has energy, and by holding onto stuff that has been hanging around for years and building up stale negative energy, is like wading through a swamp of clutter that serves no purpose.

If there are clothes in your wardrobe that you haven't worn for a year or so, consider getting rid of them. Six months ago, I came across a suit I bought for my wedding forty years ago. Perhaps I should have given it to a theatrical costumier - it would be ideal for a play set in the suit's era!

Clearing stuff out made me feel as though a weight had been lifted off my shoulders. By decluttering, we are making room for new positive energy to come into our lives. That is in part why, when we go on holiday, we feel good, as we are also taking a break from the negative energy that clutter accumulates. When we have fewer possessions, we value those that we have.

Imagine you were about to move to a smaller home so there would be a limit to what you could take with you. Take a pen and paper and without looking around, make a list of the items you would want to take. Then take your list, walk around the house and see what you have left off the list. Do you really need those items? We have become a nation of hoarders - look at the pictures of people who are refugees; some have only what they can carry. During my time in the Royal Navy, we had to evacuate refugees from Aden during a civil war, and when we took the people off the beaches, they were just glad to still be alive. Life is much more than material possessions.

Avoid or reduce the number of pictures of people on children's bedroom walls, as they can carry the energy of the people they depict. When it comes to de-cluttering children's rooms, you may need to use a bit of psychology, because children will be more attached to their possessions than an adult, even when they no longer play with them. Nevertheless, unless the bedroom is Dr. Who's Tardis, something will need to go. If it is a young child, you can say that there are lots of poor children who have no toys at all, and maybe they could use some of the toys that your own children no longer play with.

My friend Tania told me she decluttered her children's cupboards immediately before Christmas and their birthdays, as the children were less likely to become upset at the loss of their old stuff when they knew that new toys would soon come along. Having said this, Tania's middle-aged daughter, Amber, still has her very precious and now very worn-out old dolly, while Tania herself, who is in her mid-seventies, still has a small teddy bear that her father bought her when she was six years old! Sometimes things hold important memories that in themselves are healing, due to their link with loving people and happy times in the past. So, maybe think a little before chucking out everything in the house!

Food and Nutrition

The way we eat is important for a healthy life, and our relationship with food is fascinating. You may notice some people put on weight when they retire or change job. A good example would be that of a postman who walks five miles every day, as he will need to eat a goodly amount of food to replace the energy he uses. The day after he retires, he is likely to carry on eating the same quantity of food, because that is what he is used to and it is what his body tells him that it needs. As the weeks, months and years pass, he will put on weight unless he realises the need for change.

We tend to eat at regular times and not always when we are hungry, as I know from personal experience. I was in the Royal Navy for thirty years, and my last posting was as an Instructor for new recruits at the Naval Training Centre H M S Raleigh. I would take the young recruits on five-mile runs and over assault courses; the final stage of their training was a weekend on Dartmoor, trekking up and down the Tors (hills) with heavy backpacks. Needless to say, I had to lead by example and I would not expect them to do anything I didn't or couldn't do. Two years after I left the Navy, I had gained two stone in weight. The problem is that we don't wake up one morning and feel overweight – just like old age, weight creeps up on us.

Sensible eating could include the occasional day of fasting. History tells us that fasting has been used to recover good health for thousands of years. Hippocrates, Socrates and Plato all recommended fasting for health, and in the Bible, Moses and Jesus fasted for forty days for spiritual renewal. More recently, Mahatma Gandhi fasted for twenty-one days to promote respect and compassion between people of different religions.

16: A Healthy Lifestyle

Orthodox Jews observe several fast days during the year for reasons of remembrance and sadness rather than for health, which shows how powerful an activity fasting is.

As a powerful therapeutic process, fasting can help people to recover from mild to severe health conditions. When we fast, the energy that is used to digest food is redirected to the healing of issues. By fasting, you will have more energy and healthier skin, and it will eliminate toxins from the body. You will re-boot your body and food will taste better. It is good to start slowly by fasting on only one day a week, and when you do break your fast, it is important that you do not over-eat. It is normal to get headaches when you start to fast; this is a result of your body removing the toxins. Even those who are on slimming diets suffer headaches at the start of the process, due to the diminished level of sugars in the body at that time.

> *Long periods of fasting are not recommended without prior medical advice*

You are what you eat, so eating the right food is important for a healthy lifestyle. The food you buy from the supermarket is not nearly as nice as the food you can grow on your local allotment or in your vegetable patch. Food production is a business, and the food producers need to get the most profit they can from their crops. So, they plant the seeds closer together, which means that the nutrients in the soil are being shared by more plants, and to overcome this, they add fertilisers and chemicals to the earth.

Energy Healing in Focus

Supermarkets need foodstuffs to have a long shelf life, so again more chemicals are sprayed or waxy stuff is coated onto the outside of fruits. Pesticides are toxic and are not helpful to wildlife, while organic pesticides are expensive. One can buy organic food, and while it is unfortunately more expensive, it is better for you and it tastes better.

Take-away food is another story. How much chicken is there in a chicken nugget? The American Journal of Medicine published a paper on chicken nuggets, which showed that they could not tell muscle from fat, blood vessels, internal organs, skin, cartilage, bones and nerves. The meat content was as low as forty per cent. The chicken nuggets are only a chicken by-product, while the rest is salt, sugar and fat.

Some chicken breasts on sale in leading supermarkets are pumped up with water and additives that make up nearly a fifth of the meat. The cheaper ranges of frozen chicken have additives such as phosphates incorporated to stop the water from flooding out during cooking, and dextrose, a sugar, is added to mask the saltiness of the raw material. Chicken bulked up with water is also widely used in fast food restaurants, while cooked chicken from supermarkets is often marketed as "tasty", which means it has been injected with sugar.

The best place to buy your meat is from the local butcher

Beside our food, we should avoid excessive amounts of alcohol and smoking. Listen to your body - it will tell you what is good and what is harmful.

Seventeen: A Miscellany of Methods

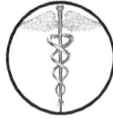

SOMETHING OLD

Ayurveda

The roots of Ayurveda reach back into pre-history, so it could be the oldest form of medicine in existence. It comes from the Indus Valley in India, which was one of the cradles of civilization. One might call it a combined holistic way of promoting good health, as it encompasses surgery, herbal medicines, yoga, meditation, diet, weight regulation, exercise and hygiene. It is mainly plant-based so it doesn't really come into the realm of Energy Healing.

SOMETHING NEW

Homeopathy

Homeopathy is based on giving the patient a distillation of chemical that has been diluted to the point where only its energy footprint remains. There is a great deal of argument as to whether it has any relevance or not, but it certainly has its adherents, with Queen Elizabeth II being one of them.

Hypnotherapy

In the case of hypnotherapy, the therapist puts the patient into a relaxed state, where he can impress ideas that will help the patient to lose weight, stop smoking or change his behaviour in some other beneficial way. One interesting aspect of this is healing otherwise pointless fears and phobias that originate in past lives. For instance, someone who is unreasonably terrified of water might have drowned in a previous life.

Kinesiology and Aura Soma

One method of kinesiology is used to identity allergies, intolerances or ailments. In the case of allergy or intolerance, the patient holds a small jar containing the item in his hand while stretching his arm out to his side. The therapist tries to push the arm down, while asking the person to resist the pressure. If the arm goes down quickly, it shows that the person is intolerant of the item while, if the arm stays up, he isn't.

This can be used alongside Aura Soma, whereby the patient makes a choice from a case of small bottles containing coloured oils and water. He holds the little bottle in his right hand while the therapist tries to push his arm down. This helps the therapist to identify the mental or physical problem that is bothering the patient.

Most Kinesiology doesn't involve any arm-pressing, just a special programme of exercise and movement, which obviously promotes good health.

Light, Space, Direction and Spirituality

Normally after I give an Energy Healing session, I ask the clients whether they saw any colours while the healing was taking place. Most people say they see blue and green, which seem to be the most popular colours, but some describe a warm bright light, as if the sun was filling the room, and they express surprise when they open their eyes and realise that the room is fairly dark.

The bright light that we see is beyond our normal physical senses, but it is still real. If what we are seeing isn't in the material world, then it must be in another dimension, which means that we view it through our mind or higher self. Notice, I said mind and not brain, because there is a difference. The brain is a physical organ located in the head; it serves as the centre of the nervous system and it controls the other organs in the body.

On the other hand, the mind has an awareness or consciousness of the way we feel at a given time. The mind can be influenced by the senses of sight, touch, hearing, smell and taste, but it is more than these things alone. When we sleep, our mind can act independently from our physical body, so when we are in a meditative state, we use the mind or the higher self to connect with, or become aware of, our spirituality.

Sometimes a spiritual occurrence can reverse this process, and it can have a weird effect on the mind and the way that it works. The following story shows what I mean.

I recall a time when I attended a Holy Fire Master Teacher course. The course took place over a weekend in Chalice Well in Glastonbury. Chalice Well is situated at the foot of Glastonbury Tor, and legend has it that this is the place to which Joseph of Arimathea brought the cup that was used at the Last Supper. The place has a very special feel. Besides me, there were five other Reiki Masters present, including a Buddhist Nun. When we meditated together in a circle, our combined energy, together with the location, resulted in a very spiritual feeling. When we finished the meditation and I opened my eyes, I felt disorientated. During the meditation, I felt as if I had been facing the direction of the Tor, but in reality, I was facing away from it and towards the town. While meditating, my higher self or mind had turned. I remember speaking to a trance healer who confirmed my impression by saying that when he came out of trance, he would often be facing a different direction than he expected.

So In this Book We Have Discovered...
Charismatic American Church ministers who do the "laying on of hands" as a kind of show business event probably don't do any harm, but it takes more than one session to achieve anything, and the less of the Healer's ego that is involved, the better the result.

Whether the Energy Healer uses a well-known method or an unusual one such as Pranic Healing, Tong Ren Therapy, Zero Balancing or Thought Field Therapy, he is using his or her knowledge and energy for the benefit of the patient. In most cases, the therapist will link to his higher consciousness, his spirit guides, the universe or a particular religious deity. It all helps to bring about the small miracle of starting the process of emotional or physical healing and that can't be bad, can it?

Conclusion

Energy Healing in Focus

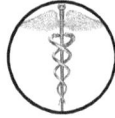

Intention is such an important part of the healer's role that I thought I would expand on it a bit.

For the past eighteen months, I have sent distant healing to a friend of mine who has cancer, and I have been doing this every Monday night at nine o'clock. Unfortunately, last week she passed away, but as a healer you have to accept these setbacks. You may feel that your healing was not good enough or strong enough, or that you could have done better, but you must remember the "healer" does not actually provide the healing, only the pathway that enables the healing to take place.

As healers, we do our best, but we can't allow ourselves to become attached to the outcome of the healing – and in many ways, this is the hardest part of being a healer. If we assumed it was us ourselves who had the power to heal, we would then think that we are better than God, Spirit, Source, Divine Power, the Universe or whatever you choose to call it. Having said all this, it is natural for us to be delighted when we see positive results from our efforts, and that is as it should be.

There is also the bigger issue of why some people do not heal, but we aren't in charge of the destiny of others and we don't know why they are being given the lesson of ill health in this life.

Conclusion

This reminds me of a story that occurred during a UK fire-fighters strike some years ago. At that time, the armed services were called in to help, and they used vintage fire engines known as "Green Goddesses" which had been built in the early 1950s. One day, a Green Goddess and a crew of sailors were called out by an old lady whose cat had got stuck up a tree. When the Green Goddess and the crew arrived, they set about putting up the ladder and rescuing the cat, and the old lady was so pleased with the rescue that she invited them in for a cup of tea and biscuits. When the crew were leaving, they accidentally ran over the cat and killed it! It seems that it was the cat's time to pass over and nothing was going to stop that happening, so while the sailors meant well, the outcome was not what they wanted or expected.

This story shows that there is no place for ego in healing, and that we are no more than an instrument to facilitate the healing that should be happening – assuming that is what is meant for the patient in question.

* * *

This book has given you a glimpse of the different forms of Energy Healing. If you are drawn to any of the methods mentioned, please contact the various organisations and federations online to find out where you can get professional training. It is easy to locate these on the internet. Before you offer your services to the public, you will need Public Liability Insurance and Professional Indemnity Insurance, and you can find this on the internet or maybe via whichever organisation you join.

I wish you the very best of health and happiness.
Des Hynes

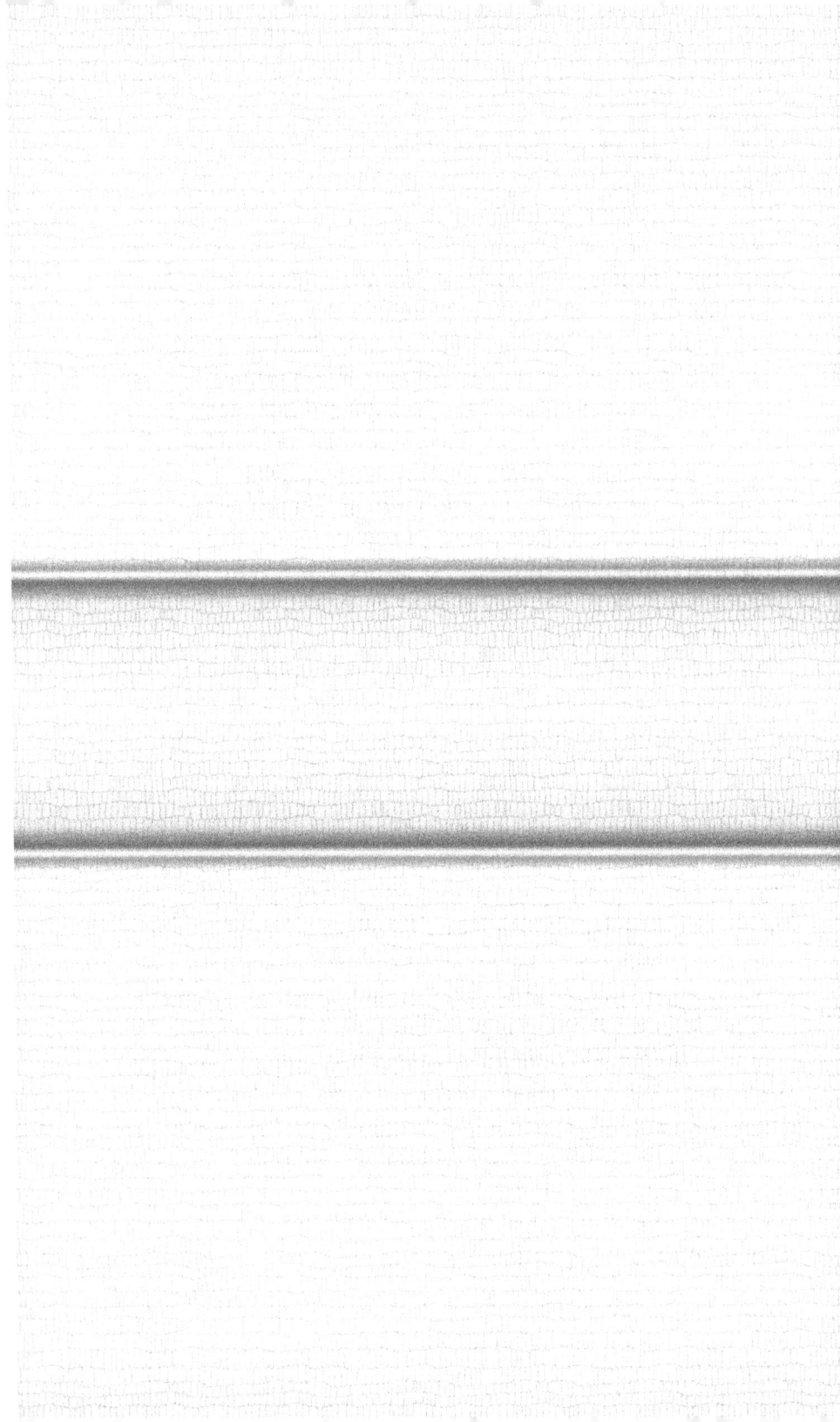

Index

Index

Index

Index

Worry 41

X
X-rays 29

Y
Yang 3
Yellow 119
Yin 3
Yin and Yang 78
Yin and Yang energy 72

Z
Zero Balancing 137

Lightning Source UK Ltd.
Milton Keynes UK
UKHW02f0015050218
317352UK00004B/14/P